Courtney's Legacy

COURTNEY'S LEGACY

A Father's Journey

—⟶⟵—

GEORGE CANTOR

Taylor Trade Publishing

Published by Taylor Trade Publishing
4720 Boston Way
Lanham, MD 20706

Distributed by National Book Network

Library of Congress Cataloging-in-Publication Data
Cantor, George, 1941–
    Courtney's legacy : a father's journey / George Cantor.
        p. c.m.
    ISBN 0-87833-260-x (cloth)
    1. Bereavement—Psychological aspects. 2. Children—Death—Psychological
aspects. 3. Parent and child. 4. Cantor, George, 1941––—Family 5. Fathers—United
States—Biography. I. Title.

BF575.G7 C35 2001
155.9'37—dc21   2001027504

    ∞™ The paper used in this publication meets the minimum requirements of
American National Standard for Information Sciences—Permanence of Paper for
Printed Library Materials, ANSI/NISO Z39.48-1992.

Manufactured in the United States of America.

To the friends who loved her:
Bekah, Jen, Karen, Nicole, Rachel, and Jessica

PREFACE

I did not set out to write a self-help book. I'm not that smart. I don't have all the answers.

But I thought it might be useful for others who have lost a child, or know someone who has, to share what we went through and how we dealt with it.

And what we took away from the ordeal, too, because that is a critical consideration. Our lives have changed in countless ways since the death of our beautiful, bright, funny eighteen-year-old daughter Courtney at the University of Michigan in the fall of 1998.

Not all of the changes were negative. Some of them have made us stronger people, who have learned to hold the gifts of life more dearly than we had before.

Courtney's death was national news, featured on the CBS program *48 Hours* and widely discussed on every campus in the country. She fell from her sixth-floor dormitory window after attending a fraternity party at which drinks were served illegally and the date-rape drug GHB was used.

So this book is also intended as a wake-up call for parents who may be lulled into believing that some of our nation's finest universities actually mean what they say when they promise to safeguard the well-being of their youngest students. Don't make the mistake of believing these institutions for a minute. We did, to our regret.

This book also gives us a way to express our love and thanks to the friends and family who took our hands as we walked down the darkest path of our lives. Our love and thanks also go out to Courtney's legion of friends. She touched their lives profoundly, and they miss her as deeply as we do. Most of all, this book is dedicated to the Temple Israel minyan group, who restored us to life.

Closure, to use that odious TV news term, is impossible. Children are wishes made flesh, and their loss will remain a defining part of your life. Nor do I claim to speak for the experience of every parent who has lost a child. The wrenching upheaval is common to every loss at any age, but each situation is different.

I have come to believe, however, that by refusing to withdraw from life, or refusing to push the memory of your child into some dimly lit and rarely visited corner of your mind, but instead celebrating life instead, parents who have lost children may still prevail.

We have prevailed. The loss has been immense, but out of our sorrow we have found a saving measure of joy.

GEORGE CANTOR
October 2000

Courtney's Legacy

CHAPTER I

———⌀———

Writers look for foreshadowing. It's a little game authors play to try and convince readers that the world makes sense.

Foreshadowing promises, after all, that the shape of things to come can be discerned from a slightly adjusted perception. Nothing so terrible will happen that hasn't been previously signified, if only we were given the wit to see.

Foreshadowing is used in all the very best novels and screenplays, and comfort can be taken from it. The alternative possibility—that life may simply be a series of disconnected accidents—is much too hard to accept.

So, as a writer, I look back for a clue. Was there some

shadow I had failed to notice, some whisper of disaster that would have warned me about the phone call from the University of Michigan Hospital?

The message reached me in the city room of the *Detroit News*, where I had been a columnist for twenty years. As soon as I walked into my office that bright October morning, the paper's operator told me about an emergency call waiting. Journalists grow accustomed to emergency calls. Usually, they're nothing of the sort. Someone's idea of an emergency is typically your waste of time.

"Do you have a daughter named Courtney attending the University of Michigan?" asked a woman's voice at the other end of the line.

"Yes," I said. "Yes, I do."

The University Hospital? Oh, shit! My mind raced through the possibilities. The worst I could come up with was that she had been raped.

"Her name is Courtney Lisa Cantor?"

"That's right."

"There's been an accident."

Oh, Courtney, you klutz. What have you stumbled into now? She had tripped and banged her knee on a parked car while running on campus a few days before. She was always crashing into things, ever since she was a toddler. A fractured ankle on a sled. A mashed finger in a door hinge. A broken nose running around like an idiot in a friend's basement during an electrical blackout. Now she was almost nineteen years old, a college freshman, and she still couldn't get it straight.

"She fell from her residence hall last night," said the voice.

This news is starting to sound bad. What is it this time? Broken leg? Collarbone?

"What condition is she in?" I asked.

There was no perceptible pause.

"She didn't survive," was the answer.

I felt my throat suddenly drop to the region of my kidneys. There was a sense of all the air rushing from my lungs, of time crashing in on me from the ceiling.

Three words spoken into a telephone receiver, and everything in life had been turned upside down.

"Oh, my God," was all that I could manage to get out in response. The soothing telephone voice cautioned me to sit down for a few moments before I drove to Ann Arbor, forty-five minutes away.

"Oh, my God," I repeated. *How could this happen to my little girl?*

———◇———

So. About the foreshadowing.

Maybe it was the day we moved her into the room at Mary Markley Hall, the university dormitory, barely six weeks ago. Had the shadow fallen there?

I had planned to say good-bye to her before driving home that evening by repeating a little ritual we had always run through when I would drop her off at grade school.

"See ya' later, alligator," she would say before opening the car door.

"After awhile, crocodile," I would, of course, respond.

Then she'd give me a quick kiss on the cheek and say, "I love you, alligator."

"I love you, crocodile."

Only then would she slide from the front seat and go on her way to class.

So when it came time to drop her off at Markley that evening, I thought I'd revive the alligator routine as a way of working through a tough moment. But that wasn't how it came out.

Courtney had choreographed the entire day as if directing the invasion of a small republic.

She had wanted to live in Markley. It was known as the cool dorm. Lots of kids from New York City traditionally lived there, people from backgrounds similar to hers. They would be in the same classes and rush the same sororities.

She already knew several of them from an orientation course she attended in June, and from chat rooms, where they had sought one another out.

Courtney was the consummate angle player. If extra school assignments could be done to nail down an A, she was on them like a shark. If a cushy job turned up that added to her summer stash, she was first in line.

She knew that if she signed up for the 21st Century Program, she would automatically be assigned to Markley. This program was a special course for freshmen, designed, ostensibly, to introduce them to situations and dilemmas they would encounter in college life and beyond. So as soon as the acceptance came through from the university, her application went out for 21st Century. The program administrator told us later that it was the first one she had received, and Courtney's photograph was the first that went up on the office bulletin board.

Once Markley was secured, the question of a roommate arose. Courtney would take no chances with this, either. Her older sister, Jaime, then a senior at U-M, had been more passive as a freshman and allowed the university to assign her a roomie.

She wound up with a corker, a young woman who invited boys into the room at 3 A.M. and then ended up not speaking to Jaime by the start of the second semester. Jaime finally had to transfer to another residence hall.

Courtney watched and learned. Roommate problems would definitely not happen to her.

The search began six months before classes started, and through mutual friends she managed to locate a likely candidate. Marni Golden came from the suburbs of Minneapolis, and the preliminary long distance and e-mail contacts were promising.

But this courting ritual was far more elaborate. Both of them took high school senior trips to Cancun in April, with a one-day overlap in their stays. Their attempt at a meeting fell through when Courtney managed to go to the wrong lobby of Marni's hotel. Despite nine years at summer camp, she was never too keen on navigational skills.

The meeting eventually took place the following month in Ann Arbor, when Marni's parents, Marshall and Nancy, came in for the graduation of her older brother. We all met for breakfast and could see within minutes that the girls were a match. Not only did they look vaguely alike, but even the pictures of their friends in the photo albums they brought along looked alike.

Marni came back to the university in July for her orientation course, and afterwards my wife, Sherry, brought her back to our home, in the suburbs of Detroit. Courtney had laid out a massive shopping expedition to buy all the things that would be needed for their dorm room, from storage shelves to a microwave oven to a minirefrigerator.

"We started going through the stores and I asked myself, 'Who is this girl?'" Marni recalls. "I'd never met anyone in my life as organized as her. She knew exactly what she was going to get and where she was going to get it. She definitely had a plan."

One of the primary considerations was the care and dressing of their loft. Michigan, like most large universities, has serious space problems in its residential halls. In some recent years, the overflow had to be quartered temporarily in corridors or in spaces intended as common areas. The situation isn't quite as bad as at Boston University, where many freshmen are put up for an entire semester at a nearby Howard Johnson's motel. But there was usually a crunch.

Even when an entering student landed a room, however, it was no great prize. Units originally designed as singles—and very small singles at that—were now claustrophobic doubles, and onetime doubles were triples.

With the advent of the computer age, requiring placement of a laptop and desk in these rooms, the squeeze was even tighter. Most of the rooms had all the charm and livability of the state pen. As an incentive to go straight in later life, they were ideal. As one's space for the academic year, though, they fell somewhere short of cozy.

But college students are an inventive bunch, and for years most of them had solved the problem by placing lofts in their rooms. These elevated bunk beds cleared the floor area for additional living space. In fact, a lively market in lofts ensued on move-in days at the dorms. Vendors with stacks of precut wood stationed themselves nearby, looking for all the world like foresters at a medieval fair. Their going rate for installing a loft was around $150.

Jaime had been placed in a residence hall that opened in 1915, the same year my father was born. And my father was in much better shape than that building. Her loft, which had been arranged for by the problematic roommate, looked like something washed up from the *Andrea Doria.*

Markley was of more recent vintage, in a cluster of dorms just to the east of the main U-M campus, in an area known as The Hill. On many of Markley's floors, the university was installing modular furniture that would remove the need for lofts and brighten up the environment. This process had yet to reach the sixth floor, where Courtney and Marni had been assigned.

So serious thought went into the best placement of the lofts in the tiny room, and their installation was all diagrammed beforehand. Courtney thought of everything.

Move-in day was September 1. The university allows freshmen to move into their dorms only on designated days. Otherwise, madness and gridlock would consume the streets of Ann Arbor. Move-in days aren't quite as bad as an ordinary football Saturday, when more than one hundred thousand people try to pile into the town and roads are backed up for miles. Even so, they are an ordeal, with parking almost nonexistent.

We borrowed a pickup truck for the big event. Courtney had us positioned in front of her dorm at 8 A.M., the very moment the parking lot opened. Marni and her family had spent the night at a nearby hotel and already were unloaded and ready to go.

Markley has a somewhat unique floor plan. From the parking area, one enters the building's third floor. Then it is necessary to take elevators up or down to reach the other residence floors. Courtney's sixth-floor room was only three flights up from the front of the building.

From the rear, however, where her room faced, Markley was a full six stories high, directly above a service entrance and concrete driveway where heavy equipment could be unloaded.

The chief attribute of her room was the view. Its windows offered a sweeping vista across the grounds of the University Hospital to North Campus, and then to the hills beyond.

"This will really be beautiful in October when the leaves turn," I said. That was all that occurred to me when I first walked into the room. *How lovely it would be to wake up to this scene in autumn.*

Aesthetic considerations interested no one else, though. All the stuff needed to be moved in and directions given to the loft-builders. As the structure went up, Marshall and I were kept busy moving the beds that came with the room down to a basement storage area and then coming back with mattresses for the lofts. That activity took us out of the way, which was probably the main purpose of the errand. It was hot work, and we were grateful for the fan that had been placed on the window ledge and which circulated some slight breath of air through the tiny space.

By the time we were finished schlepping the beds around, the lofts were up. They were placed on either side of the room as one entered it, with the heads pointed toward the windows. A crossbeam ran across the room's width so that a ladder could slide back and forth from one loft to the other. Otherwise, getting down took a bit of a jump.

Move-in was finished by 4 P.M. We then posed for pictures, Courtney and Marni and the two sets of parents, all stretched out on a futon that had been placed under Courtney's loft, sweaty and giggling and very grateful that the move had been accomplished with a minimum of strain. Just as Courtney had planned.

We all drove over to one of Ann Arbor's student landmarks, the Cottage Inn, for pizza. Both Courtney and Marni had invited other friends, and Jaime, never one to pass on a free meal, showed up, too, with her boyfriend. The gang of us took up a long table in an upstairs dining room.

Then it was time to go. Sherry does not handle good-byes well, so she went with Jaime back to the house our daughter was renting on the far side of campus. I would drop Courtney off at the dorm before rejoining Sherry for the drive back home.

Nighttime was setting in by the time we reached the front of Markley. I stopped the car and was about to start the alligator routine when Courtney grabbed me in a ferocious hug. She was barely five feet tall and weighed a bit over one hundred pounds, but she was an athlete and could be surprisingly strong.

We hugged for a long minute, so tightly that speaking became difficult. I think the fierce embrace was a way for her to say, "I love you," without actually using the words.

Finally, I managed to murmur, "Don't do anything stupid."

Why I chose those words for my good-bye, I still cannot explain. Had I noticed something that had registered only in my subconscious, but close enough to the surface to come bubbling out as a caution? If so, what was it?

I just don't know, and I can't even remember how she responded to this abrupt warning. She just turned to the door of the pickup, eager to begin her great college adventure, and was gone.

She had forty-six days to live.

CHAPTER 2

—⚬—

Burying a child is one of the most common events in human history. In many eras, it merely fell within the expected course of life. Religious practices, disease, poverty, warfare—all claimed the very young as their chief victims.

Only in comparatively recent years has the loss of a child been regarded as the supreme calamity, a shocking distortion in the normal progression of life, an anguish too deep for words.

Enclosed within the folds of human myth lies the belief that the sacrifice of a child is a reasonable response to frightening and overpowering events. Loss of a child is the toll that fate exacts for being human, to love what death can touch.

One of the terrible ironies of our times is also that no sooner had the old dangers been vanquished than entirely new menaces made childhood deadly again.

Cars. Guns. Suicide. A pervasive culture of substance abuse on high school and college campuses. These terrors now haunt the dreams of parents, exchanging new nightmares for old.

Among the ancient peoples in the Middle Eastern cradle of civilization, the king's son was usually chosen to die. Philo of Byblus, in his *History of the Jews,* wrote about the custom for the ruler to give his son as a sacrifice "for the whole people, as a ransom offered to the avenging demons."

The Old Testament's Book of Kings notes that when the Israelites were besieging the King of Moab, he took his eldest son and used him as a burnt offering upon the city walls.

Judaism grew up in an epoch and a region where child sacrifice was a universally accepted form of religious magic. Consider the significance of the story of Abraham's near sacrifice of his son, Isaac, in Genesis. Modern readers find this one of the most disturbing stories in the Bible. The willingness with which the old man is ready to take the boy's life at the command of God is met with horror and revulsion. Some readers perceive Abraham as a zealot, a religious nut. Jonestown without the Kool-Aid.

But Abraham's hand is stayed by an angel of the Lord, which is the whole point. This religion does not demand the sacrifice of a child to appease an angry deity. Abraham's refrainment is one of the great turning points in human ethics. While children were still at risk through the usual course of events, their deaths were no longer to be part of a deliberate ritual, which is among the essential first distinctions between paganism and Western religion.

In the Middle Ages, an era consumed by the idea of death as a public and personal statement, even the children of nobility were customarily not buried on church grounds. The death of children was simply regarded as too commonplace to allow for taking up scarce space in holy ground. They were instead buried in a cemetery plot, the resting place of the poor.

The large families that were common for centuries in rural areas were insurance policies against the predictable loss of children. The unfortunate peasant who halted the process of procreation too soon ran a sizeable risk of leaving himself with insufficient hands to work the land and, eventually, to support him as he aged.

Medieval folk tales compiled by the Brothers Grimm

are full of images of children facing death. The most enduring, of course, is Hansel and Gretel, abandoned and starving in the dark woods. They are saved from death and the wicked witch only by Gretel's ingenuity. But the fairy tale reflects a real memory of famine, cultural upheaval, and the experiences of families who did not live happily ever after.

On the American frontier, historian Lewis O. Saum notes the practice of leaving babies unnamed—not only unbaptized but unnamed—until they reached the age of one year. He concludes that because death was so common, parents used this practice to insulate themselves from death's inevitability.

Letters home announcing the birth of a new child were usually accompanied by a statement of disavowal. "But how long we shal be allowed to keep him is inknown to us," was a rather typical phrase, writes Saum.

Photographers in rural communities developed a standard protocol for taking pictures of infants in their tiny coffins. In his best-selling study of one such cameraman, *Wisconsin Death Trip,* writer Michael Lesy found plate after plate of such pictures in the studio at Black River Falls, an unsettling record of how easily children were swept away.

Diphtheria, whooping cough, measles, polio, tuberculosis, as well as a dozen other diseases to which children were susceptible, raged through the nineteenth century. Even as technological progress was raising to undreamed-of levels the standard of material well-being in the middle class, their children could be taken from them at any time, and they were powerless to prevent it.

Poems about the death of children were standard fare even in books intended for children. *McGuffey's New Fourth Eclectic Reader,* the basic reading text in most American schools in the late nineteenth century, contains a work entitled "What Is Death?"

Its opening lines depict a child speaking to its mother. "Mother, how still the baby lies! / I cannot hear his breath. / I cannot see his laughing eyes; / They tell me this is death."

Such material was regarded as a good way to prepare children for an event they would almost surely witness.

Even the First Home in the land was no sanctuary. When Abraham Lincoln lost his ten-year-old son, Willie, to a fever in February 1862, in the midst of the Civil War, the White House was plunged into deepest mourning. Always a melancholy man, Lincoln was described as being despondent for months afterward, and his wife very nearly went mad from grief. Another child had died as an infant in Illinois and the death of Willie, wrote Lincoln biographer Carl Sandburg, was as if they had lost their first son a second time.

One of those who wrote to Lincoln at this time was former president Franklin Pierce. Just before leaving New Hampshire to begin his term in office in 1853, Pierce had seen his son killed in a railroad accident. His biographers say that Pierce was left numb by the shock, and his presidency was marred by his inability to move decisively on any issue.

The writer who read the public's emotions most masterfully was Charles Dickens. His description of the death of Little Nell in *The Old Curiosity Shop* wrung uncontrollable sobs from Victorian audiences at its publication and when the author read passages aloud during public appearances. Almost all of these families had been touched by such a death.

"When Death strikes down the innocent and the young," he wrote, "for every fragile form from which he lets the panting spirit flee, a hundred virtues rise, in shapes of mercy, charity and love, to walk the world and bless it."

Out of this mixture of material wealth and the ever-present chance of death at an early age, the Victorians created their enduring, sentimentalized version of childhood. The era produced many of the great classics of children's literature and left a legacy of childhood as a time to be treasured, a fantasy world of innocence and joy.

But just below the surface there is always the skull. The death of Beth in *Little Women*. Only after he sees Tiny Tim's empty chair is Scrooge transformed in *A Christmas Carol*. What is Peter Pan's Never-Never Land, the image of an eternal playground, far beyond "the second star to the right and straight on 'til morning," where one can never grow old? This space is a child's view of heaven without the dying.

The ghosts of absent children haunt the imaginations of the era's finest writers, from Henry James and *The Turn of the Screw* to Rudyard Kipling's classic short story, "They." Their spirits skip just out of sight and are forever young.

Kipling, however, was also a staunch advocate of war as the finest testing ground of a nation's youth. He was among the most enthusiastic voices in the run-up to World War I, seeing this first and most terrible of modern wars as the best way to reclaim the manly virtues for a country growing too rich and soft.

He was echoed on this side of the Atlantic by former president Theodore Roosevelt. Both men would lose sons in the conflict and suffer greatly from the loss for the rest of their lives.

When the guns fell silent on the Western Front, the life expectancy of a child born in the United States was 54.1 years. In the next four decades, that span would be extended by an incredible sixteen years.

While average life expectancy has moved up since then, the increment is much smaller. The big statistical jump prior to 1960 reflects the triumph of medicine over childhood disease.

Vaccines, improved natal care, access to hospitals, antibiotics . . . one by one the age-old killers succumbed. When polio was added in 1955 to the list of former killers, the cloud that had darkened the lives of the Victorians appeared to be permanently dispelled. Not only would we be the wealthiest society ever to exist on Earth, our children would be the most secure.

But it didn't turn out that way. The way we live now brings new perils.

The National Center for Health Statistics charted steep declines in the death rates of children between birth and fourteen years since 1950. They are now less than half of where they stood just fifty years in the past. But from the ages of fifteen to twenty-four, the rate shows just a slight dip, and for some of the 1970s it even went up slightly.

Of the 30,627 deaths in that age group in America in 1998, the year Courtney died, the one-time feared killers of young people—tuberculosis, polio, diphtheria, pneumonia—were barely on the charts among the top ten causes. But more than 70 percent were the result of accidents, homicides, and suicides.

Relocating to the suburbs meant that more teenagers would be driving for longer times over faster, more dangerous roads. The horrific rate of youth auto fatalities has caused several states to raise age restrictions for a driver's license and limit its use to daylight hours.

The flood of drugs into middle-class America that began in the 1960s placed more young people at risk, especially since this new form of recreation accompanied a breakdown in the restraining influence of the family.

The urban gun culture had claimed so many lives by the 1990s that the National Centers for Disease Control and Prevention moved to classify firearms deaths as a health epidemic. In 1998 it was the leading cause of death overall for males between the ages of fifteen and twenty-four.

Parental organizations were formed to try and respond to these threats to children. The mission of Mothers Against Drunk Driving (MADD) is to stiffen the sentencing laws for convicted drunk drivers. Save Our Sons and Daughters (SOSAD) organized to stop the wave of drive-by shootings and casual gang slaughter that has invaded the cities.

They mourn the loss of their children to a culture that had turned and devoured them.

The assurance that we had finally succeeded in shielding our children from harm has been shattered. We overcame the fear of losing our children to polio on some hot summer night only to lose them to a gun in a schoolroom. We have kept them from the carnage of the battlefield only to find it on the freeway.

We do not sacrifice children to win deliverance from the gods anymore. Our reasons aren't that good. The theme running constantly through the work of Stephen King, the most popular American novelist of the late twentieth century, is the peril, and often the death, of a small child. This motif is not a coincidence.

The unutterable grief of looking down into a coffin at the face of your child binds us to a past we thought had been left behind forever.

CHAPTER 3

The human brain can be a merciful organ. At times of great pain it covers awareness in a gauzy film, softening the edges of anguish.

My recollection of the hours that followed Courtney's death fades in and out of focus.

I remember getting into my car and yelling at her, telling her how furious I was that she had gone and died. I told her that it was simply irresponsible, unacceptable behavior.

The awful fact of death was not still capable of penetrating. It was as if, instead, I was just going off to the hospital once more and soon would see her emerge with a rueful smile on her face and yet another appendage in a cast. I knew that drill.

To actually admit the life that I had watched come into the world—cutting the umbilical cord to formally initiate it—was now over exceeded my capacity for understanding.

I did know, however, that within the hour I would have to tell my wife, and in some ways that would be even worse than the phone call I had just received.

Sherry's life already had so much loss. Her mother had passed away from a brain tumor when Sherry was not quite seven years old. She had watched her father die of a heart attack when she was twenty-three. Our two children had been her chance to restore the world that had been torn away from her.

Death had touched me only lightly. My parents, my brother—alive and in good health. Only my grandparents were gone, but that is the order of things. Courtney was named for my paternal grandmother, so that her memory would gain a degree of immortality. Now that progression, too, was shattered.

Lines from *King Lear* skittered through my mind, even though it was not my favorite Shakespeare play and I hadn't even looked at it since college. But suddenly, as if I had read it just yesterday, I heard the despairing wail of the aged king, mourning Cordelia, his daughter:

"Why should a dog, a horse, a rat have life,
And thou no breath at all? Thou'lt come no more.
Never, never, never, never, never."

One thought kept running through my mind with terrible clarity: I was thankful I was already 57 years old. That meant it wouldn't be that much longer I'd have to live with this.

Sherry was working as a substitute teacher at a high school in Walled Lake, a suburb about an hour's drive from my office. I found the classroom she was in and stood at the door unseen, watching her, knowing that in moments I would have to tell her something that would rip her life apart.

She looked up and saw me, smiled, and then realized that I should not be standing there. She stood, puzzled, and walked to the door where I waited.

If there were one moment in my entire life I would never want to relive, that would be the one.

———

When we arrived at the hospital in Ann Arbor, Jaime was waiting for us. The university had contacted her, and her boyfriend had brought her there.

She ran tearfully into our arms.

"We're still a family, aren't we?" she cried. For the third time on this worst day of my life, my heart broke.

The university representatives took us into a private room. We chose to wait there until the clergy from our temple arrived before going back to see Courtney.

The Michigan people were quick to let me know that she had been drinking at a fraternity party. She had died on the way to the hospital at about 5 A.M. A janitor at the dormitory had found her on his way to work. The best estimate, they told me, was that she had gone through the window at about 3 A.M.

Wait a minute! Through the window?

Right until that moment I had been under the impression that she had somehow fallen from the roof of the building.

The window? How was that possible? I had seen those windows on move-in day. Courtney was a tiny girl, sure, but how could she fit through those windows? It seemed inconceivable. What the hell had happened in that room?

As we talked, I tried to blot out the image of my daughter lying on the cement in her nightshirt as life ebbed from her. So coddled and pampered, and dying alone in the predawn cold. My only consolation was the probability that she had never regained consciousness and that, for all intents, she had died when she hit the pavement.

"We've called a news conference for 3 P.M.," the university provost told me.

Again I was staggered. All my journalistic instincts had deserted me. It simply never occurred to me that this was anything more than a private tragedy, my family's ordeal to face alone.

The university knew better. A death on campus is always news.

I knew most of the reporters who would be at the news conference, either from the newspaper or from television work I had done for the ABC affiliate in Detroit in the 1980s. I was back in familiar territory. This was my profession. I knew where I was again.

I took out my wallet and removed the photo of Courtney that I kept there, taken at the start of her high school senior year. She sat smiling, one leg folded under her, hand raised to her chin. She looked so happy and beautiful.

You'll need this," I said. "They'll want art."

That picture would smile from the pages of most of the state's newspapers in the next few days. Courtney was front-page news, a fact that would have pleased her immensely.

Rabbi Harold Loss arrived at the hospital half an hour after we did. His youngest daughter, Talya, had graduated from high school with Courtney. Harold and I had run into each other at the final parents' orientation there and sat together in the gym bleachers during the presentation.

Afterwards, he clapped me on the shoulder. "Well," he said, "that's it. We've done our duty. We'll never have to sit through one of those things again."

It was our paternal rite of passage. The open houses, teachers' meetings, carpooling. Almost over now. The end was in sight. We'd done our job and deserved a victory lap. We had it coming.

The week Courtney and Talya started classes in Ann Arbor, I had written a column about the sad happiness of sending your youngest off to college.

I recalled all the days when my daughters had begged

me to come out and play H-O-R-S-E on the basketball net beside the driveway. So many times I'd declined. I was so busy. Reading a book, or maybe writing one. Absorbed in a ballgame on TV. Just too tired. So many excuses. Besides, there would always be time to do it later.

Then the day comes when you're out of time; they stop calling, and then they're gone.

With the melancholy perspective of every parent, I wrote that if I could only hear their voices today, "the house hasn't been built that could keep me inside."

When Rabbi Loss saw me later that week he grabbed me in a hug. "That's the best column you've ever written," he said.

Now in two more days he would read from it while delivering the eulogy at Courtney's funeral.

We walked back to where she was. It wasn't a morgue, like you see in the cop shows on TV. It looked more like a storage area, or a receiving room in the rear of the hospital's lower floor. She was lying on a table, her body covered by a sheet.

For a wild instant, I wasn't sure it was really Courtney. Her face had always been so animated: her nose wrinkled in glee, her eyes wide as she told us another improbable tale, her smile lighting up as she greeted a friend. Every emotion seemed to run across her face twice a minute.

Now her face was still, and it just didn't look like her.

Rabbi Loss took our hands and led us in a short prayer. Afterwards, I reached out to brush a wisp of hair back from Courtney's forehead.

It was all I could do for her now.

———— ✄ ————

She had come on a holiday. Veterans Day, 1979. Technically speaking, the holiday was observed on Monday and she had arrived on Sunday. But why quibble?

I was, in fact, a little miffed at the timing. When Sherry told me we had better go to the hospital, it was halftime of a real good Rams–Bears game on TV. "Can't you hold on another hour or so?" I asked in my best dumb-husband tone. Her look would have shattered concrete.

As we rode the hospital elevator up to the birthing room, the attendant looked at Sherry's chart, and then did a double take at her in the wheelchair. "You're goin' natural?" she asked incredulously. "Oooh, girl, it's gonna hu-uuu-rt."

We laughed for years over that unsolicited disavowal of Dr. Lamaze and his method.

But Courtney came easily. The labor was uneventful—easy for me to say, of course—and I spent most of the time talking football with the doctor, much to Sherry's annoyance. As the final stage began, I checked my watch and told him that it looked as if the baby would be born close to the same time I was, at 7:08 P.M.

She came out with a rush. While I had been so overcome that I was barely able to keep standing when Jaime was born, I coolly observed Courtney emerge in all her glory. I cut the cord, the gender was ascertained, the nurses checked her over, and only then did the doctor realize he had forgotten to note the exact time of birth.

"Oh, well," he shrugged and scribbled down some numbers. I saw later that he had put it down as 7:08 P.M.

She looked like me, a handicap she managed to overcome. But she had her mother's assertiveness, her outgoing breeziness, her smile.

She laughed easily and cried nearly as often. Friends were life's treasures to her. There could never be enough of them. The success of any endeavor was measured by the number of friends she'd made from it. That was the whole point.

When she won a free party from a local recreation center, she delayed collecting on it until the start of the school year. She was just starting middle school and felt it would be a good way to bring everyone in the class together.

She wanted to go to Israel after the eleventh grade, but she deliberately chose a trip that would leave from New York City and not include kids she knew from the Detroit area. As we drove from the hotel to Newark Airport, she kept practicing the way she would introduce herself to the people on the flight, making sure her inflection and tone were perfect. She came home with a ton of new friends from all across the country.

She would grow weepily sentimental over her friends from summer camp. Her four weeks at Walden, located in northern Michigan, became the pivot of the year for her. Her room was filled with scrapbooks of camp memories.

The computer opened up entire new vistas of friendship. She contacted dozens of people who would be starting the University of Michigan at the same time she was. Many of them had attended smaller high schools and were a little intimidated by the prospect of the huge campus.

"Don't worry," Courtney had e-mailed them. "It'll be fine. And I'll be there for you. We're all in this together."

Many of them wrote later to tell us about this constant stream of encouragement coming from Courtney and how much it had helped them.

I asked Rabbi Loss to read during the eulogy the first stanza of a poem by William Wordsworth, "She Was a Phantom of Delight." The title described perfectly how I felt about Courtney. I called her Snort, a nickname she hated, because she always seemed to be running somewhere, filled with energy. She was a sprite who filled our lives with laughter.

She would make up incredible stories with a straight face and then break up when she knew that we had bitten on one again. Tucked deep inside my brain, even after seeing her body in the hospital, was the conviction that this was just another one of her tales—in incredibly bad taste, to be sure, but that had never stopped her before.

For weeks I half-expected the phone to ring and to hear her laughter at the other end of the line. "I really got you that time, Dad. You're such a loser. How could you ever fall for something like that?"

But the call never came.

CHAPTER 4

———⁂———

Courtney's friends gathered in force for the funeral on a drizzly Sunday two days after her death. Her closest high school buddies flew in from their colleges in Boston and Atlanta. Her best camp friend came in with her parents from Miami.

The mother of an Israel-trip friend made the three-hour drive from Cleveland because she knew her daughter wanted her to be there. Camp counselors drove in from Chicago. The university brought two chartered buses from Ann Arbor. The cantor of our temple, Harold Orbach, left a hospital bed, brushing aside the objections of his doctors, because he felt he had to sing the prayers at Courtney's funeral.

The friends she had dedicated her life to making filled every seat in the chapel. They stood at every open space along the walls. They overflowed into the vestibule area where the service was put on a loudspeaker. The driver of the hearse told us it was the largest funeral he could ever remember there. Police from four suburban departments were called in to handle the traffic on the drive to the cemetery.

Courtney was always pestering me to write a column about her or to name her in the dedication of a book, which I did on two occasions. *My God,* I thought, *how she would have loved this.*

When U-M President Lee Bollinger called our home on the night of Courtney's death, he said, "It takes an event like this to remind us what a close community the university is." In his eulogy, Rabbi Loss referred to "a community in mourning."

Incredibly, I thought, we had become the biggest story in the state. After an entire career of covering the news, my family and I had become the news and our community was reaching out to us.

The TV crews began arriving before dark on Friday, setting up on our front lawn to prepare reports for the eleven o'clock news. I did several interviews. I didn't know how to be the father of a dead child, but I knew all about giving interviews. Even though I was talking about my daughter's death, I felt detached, disconnected from reality, as if doing my usual commentaries on local politics or sports. For a few hours I had slipped into a professional cocoon, and I was grateful for the hiding place.

The CBS television show *48 Hours* was on the line, asking if they could send out a producer from New York to tape a preliminary interview. Columnists and longtime colleagues were writing about us. I disagreed vehemently with the take of one writer whom I had never met, and I found myself growing angry. "Who are you," I said to the newspaper in front of me, "to be writing about my family? You don't know us."

But I had done exactly that for years: writing, sometimes critically, about people I did not know. Now the roles were reversed, and I didn't like the feel of it.

I was stunned, however, at the public reaction. For two solid weeks, our mailbox at the house was filled with letters of consolation. The *News* sent more that had poured into my office at the paper.

Many of them were from celebrities whose careers had

crossed mine in the past. Athletes, TV anchors, business executives, politicians.

Most of the messages, however, were from people we didn't know, readers who felt they knew me through my columns and were compelled to tell us how they felt. We read them aloud every night, and some of them moved me so deeply that I couldn't go on speaking. The outpouring of love was unlike any other I had ever experienced. My daughter's death made me feel that my life in journalism had been validated.

The letter that affected me most came from a woman in Detroit who had often disagreed strenuously with me on articles I wrote about the city. Her letters were long and often biting. "I have disagreed with you in the past and will probably disagree with you in the future," she wrote. "But that seems so unimportant now."

At other times, Sherry and I felt that we were watching our lives rewind in slow motion. We heard from people with whom we had carelessly lost touch years ago: friends of our parents who had known us as children, my sixth-grade teacher from a Detroit elementary school that was no longer standing, the two high school teachers who had most profoundly shaped my life.

The first girl I had ever dated, thirty-eight years before, showed up at the house. We hadn't seen each other in years, but she told me that she had to be there. While the radio in 1960 had played "Will You Love Me Tomorrow," she broke my heart, and she helped repair it now.

We observed the Jewish custom of *shiva,* staying at home for a week while friends and relatives called, and then joining in prayer at sunset. The reasoning is excellent. If you are constantly surrounded by people who love you, you have less time to dwell upon your loss. Plenty of opportunity for that later.

Rabbi Loss encouraged us to spend the time telling "Courtney stories" while the memories were fresh and we were all together, so that we would never forget them.

We told all the favorites. How she had told her second-grade teacher that she was spending Thanksgiving with her grandmother who owned a candy store in Flint. There was no such grandmother, no such store, and no relatives in Flint, either. She once told her camp friends that she had forgotten to turn off the water at home and since she lived in a house that was seven stories high there was the chance of one spectacular flood.

We had thrown away her "security blankie" in an elaborate ritual when she started preschool, but she had sneakily cut off little strips of the thing and carried them around with her for years. She eventually disposed of the blanket cuttings but would always go to sleep holding one white sock for comfort. Jaime insisted on placing one in the coffin with her.

She went into a five-minute Elvis impersonation one time when my wife was stuck in traffic next to a driver with long sideburns and pompadoured hair.

We laughed at all the stories, and it felt good to tell them again. But Jaime came up to me at one point to say that she was worried about her grandfather.

"Poppa keeps hugging me and his eyes fill with tears and he tells me that I'm the hope of the future now," she said.

Courtney had been my dad's favorite. A picture of her taken when she was three, hair falling in untamable curls and a gleam in her sparkling eyes, held the place of honor in his wallet. He could be a gruff old guy, but Courtney knew exactly how to melt him. I prayed the loss wasn't more than he could handle.

Indulging in hagiography about the dead is natural. I

don't want to do that. Courtney was assuredly no saint. In fact, I would describe her, to use the accepted scientific terminology, as a pisser. But she made us laugh, and she knew that giving love was the single greatest imperative of life.

"We'll get through this," I kept reassuring people all week. "We're a strong family." ("We're still a family, aren't we?" Jaime had asked.) "It'll be tough, but we'll get through it."

I didn't know what I was talking about. The tough part was just beginning.

CHAPTER 5

———cℑ———

There is no easy road home from the cemetery.

Eventually, the relatives go away. The mailbox load drops to its normal size. The bills arrive and must be paid because the bank and electric company don't much care that you've lost a child.

To use the hideous TV news cliché, you've got to get on with your life.

I will now state the obvious: This is impossible.

When a parent dies, you may have the consolation of looking back and saying, "I will miss her, but she had a long and fulfilling life." There is no such thing as an easy death for the survivors at any stage of life, but one can come to it with a certain degree of acceptance.

That approach forms the basis of Dr. Jack Kevorkian's philosophy, if you can call it that. The conclusion of a life is a perfectly natural function, and the one who lives it should make the call on when and under what conditions he gives it up. Each person earns the right to determine his or her own end.

But with a child there are no such comforts, only might-have-beens.

Someone asked me what field of work I thought Courtney would have entered. I honestly had no idea. Her older sister was focused on law school from the day she entered Michigan. But Courtney tended to float around until she fixed on what she wanted, and then she was like a little bulldog until she got it. She had yet to get that fix on a profession.

So I can only wonder. Marketing? Psychology? Journalism (God forbid!)?

And that is part of the pain. The story ended before the plot really began.

She had written only three checks on the first bank account she ever opened. She never fell ridiculously in love. Never got a merit raise. Never voted for the wrong candidate. Never tasted defeat.

"Wishes are children," wrote Stephen Sondheim, in an exquisite song from the show *Into the Woods*. But the reverse is just as true. Your children become an extension of your own dreams, even the fulfillment of old wishes that had come to nothing. So the death of a child is truly a foretaste of your own.

Losing a child to death is an amputation without benefit of anesthesia because part of yourself now is gone.

A study at Boston's Dana-Farber Cancer Institute, published in 2000, indicated that children with a terminal illness frequently endure more pain and suffering than necessary, because parents refuse to let them go.

"The tremendous stakes involved in saving the life of a child make both parents and caregivers reluctant to abandon the curative approach," wrote the *New England Journal of Medicine* in an editorial response. "Thus the continuation of aggressive care is encouraged even if there is little or no realistic hope of a favorable outcome."

The parents won't surrender their wishes. It's just too damn hard.

In no way would I try to minimize the effect of watching your child die of cancer, slipping away from you day by day. But at least those parents are able to prepare themselves. They are braced for grief. It does not drop on them without warning from a brilliant October sky.

I knew that dealing with the aftermath of Courtney's funeral would be difficult for Sherry. We agreed that she would enter therapy as soon as possible.

She would wake up every morning at exactly 5 A.M., the time Courtney died. Then she would get up and try to struggle through the day before gratefully collapsing of exhaustion at about 9 at night.

Going back to work was out of the question for her. Her friends conspired to keep her occupied with an endless round of lunches, walks, shopping trips—inconsequential business to move her through the daylight hours and give her mind somewhere to go.

But talking was becoming difficult for us. An overheard phrase, a piece of music on the radio, a well-meaning remark from a friend would send her into tears, and I felt powerless to help her. Friends invited us to their vacation home in northern Michigan, and one night they showed a taped movie they thought would amuse us. It was *Sliding Doors,* with Gwyneth Paltrow. Near the end of the film, the heroine suffers a terrible injury by tumbling down a flight of stairs.

Sherry rushed from the room crying while our friends

apologized in mortification. "I forgot all about that scene," said the wife. Most people would have, but it cut too close for us.

I knew that work would be my therapy. I was just starting the research on a new book, *Bad Guys in American History*. So I would go to the office and keep busy writing columns and editorials, and then come home to get on the Internet or thumb through volumes on villainy from the library. I found that the evil works of Jesse James, Blackbeard, and their cohorts was a good antidote to the numbing grief that coursed through me whenever I stopped to think. Better not to think.

It was Jaime who stunned me, because I didn't see it coming. In recent years, an edgy rivalry had grown between the two sisters. Courtney let no one intrude on her turf, and Jaime, a far more passive personality, was sometimes hurt by Courtney's reluctance to allow her to be the big sister.

The rivalry worsened when Jaime came home from school breaks at Ann Arbor. On one notable occasion, she insisted on plugging in her own answering machine to their shared phone line. The first time the phone rang, it blew out Courtney's machine and her outrage was unconfined.

But after Courtney started school at Michigan, a change occurred. Instead of being a rival, Jaime was the one who knew the ropes in Ann Arbor, someone to lean on for advice and an occasional meal. She was permitted to be the big sister, and Jaime loved it.

Now she would be going back to the campus where her sister had died. It was too much for her. She didn't want to leave. She wanted to be a little girl again, safe in her parents' house where terrible things did not happen.

Jaime was also very conscious that she was now the entire focus of our concern. In my father's words, she had become our sole hope for the future, which was more than she was ready to deal with. Who could?

A close friend of ours lost her young brother in a drowning at summer camp. From that time on, she said, until she left home to get married, she was conscious of her mother's eyes upon her. No words, just the terrible watching. It was understandable, of course, but the constant observation left her with a sense of unease that lasted for years. At least the film hero of *The Truman Show* wasn't aware that the camera was constantly on him. But our friend knew.

With the efforts of several close friends and the cooperation of her professors, we did get Jaime back into class after another week. She had been a straight-A student at Michigan and was in line for what she had been working toward, a place in a top-tier law school. But that goal had become almost meaningless to her, and I hadn't understood.

Even when she returned to school, if she could not reach Sherry or me on the phone after a few hours, she became panic-stricken. There was no more assurance left in the world for any of us.

After Courtney's death we met several parents who had lost children. We hadn't sought each other out but were inevitably drawn together. "We're in the same club," one of the fathers said to me. But you should never have to pay an initiation fee that high.

Each of them had worked out their own way of grappling with their loss. One family left their son's phone connected after he died in an auto accident. It began ringing several months later, although no one had the number, and when they picked up the receiver there was no answer. Eventually, they began answering the line by using his name. They were satisfied it was his way of trying to contact them, to reassure them that everything was all right.

Another family, miraculously, had a child, although

both were in their fifties. They named her after their late son. "But I don't look forward to the day when she's old enough to ask me who the boy in all the pictures is," the father told me.

One mother told Sherry that she had left her son's room untouched and on many nights slept in his bed.

How can you fault any of this? Whatever helps you through is the right thing to do. People who talk about "getting on with your life" and "closure" are simply babbling. You do whatever makes life bearable again, and the rest is merely background noise.

Oddly enough, I suddenly felt the loss most when I started to travel. Travel had always been my escape. Nothing liberated me more than a drive on roads I'd never been down before.

Three months after Courtney's death, Sherry went to Phoenix with a friend. I had to fly into Albuquerque to do some work on the *Bad Guys* book and planned to join her in Arizona in four days. I looked forward eagerly to the drive as a way of getting away from familiar ground and the memories that came with it.

But from that first morning on the road, everything went wrong. I could not shake the images of Courtney from my mind. The events of that terrible weekend kept rewinding and playing back in a relentless loop.

I had to understand what had happened in that room. If I understood, then I could go back and fix it and she wouldn't have to die.

Irrational, of course. But during that long drive I sometimes felt my mind rocking within my head, threatening to burst its clamps.

The magnificent scenery of New Mexico and Arizona flashed by my window and I couldn't see it. With no one to talk to, I was trapped into reliving the nightmare over and over again.

I walked through the streets of Lincoln where Billy the Kid shot it out with his enemies, and I thought about Courtney. I visited Columbus where Pancho Villa had raided, and I thought about Courtney. I went to the OK Corral in Tombstone, and I thought about Courtney.

The days on the road by myself had become a torment instead of a release. I finally drove into Phoenix, exhausted mentally and emotionally. Never had I needed my wife more.

"How was the trip?" Sherry asked.

"Oh, fine," I said. "Just fine."

We're a strong family, I had told everyone. What I really meant is that I'm a strong person, a rock, and it was up to me to get us through this. I couldn't be weak now.

"Good," she said. "Me, too."

We could no longer talk. We had put on masks. Things were falling apart.

CHAPTER 6

———∽———

This is Sherry's chapter, written in her own words and voice.

———∽———

When my father died, and people came over to the house to pay their condolences, one close friend of my family was just beside herself. She was weeping, carrying on terribly. I was touched that my dad had meant that much to her.

As it turned out, she was in mourning for her dog, which had died a few days before. She couldn't get over it.

I'll never forget how furious I was that in the middle

of my grief over losing my father, this woman was carrying on over an animal. I love dogs. Snickers has been a fixture in our house for ten years. Courtney named him "Snickers" because we picked him up from the shelter when all her Halloween treats were still piled high in the pantry.

But, after all, relatives and dogs are different. At least, I think they are.

The day after Courtney died, while I was still numb, a high school classmate of mine, who is now a rabbi, came over to the house and took me and George aside.

"Over the next few days," he said, "people are going to say a lot of dumb things to you. Things that will make you angry. But you've got to understand it's because they don't know what to say and feel they've got to say something. Be patient. Don't get upset. They are only trying to comfort you."

That was some of the best advice we received in those first few days, and I only wish I could have taken it. But I couldn't help it.

When someone would come up to me and say, "I know how you must feel," I wanted to scream at them, "No, you don't. How could you? Unless you have lost the child you carried for nine months, and raised for eighteen years, how can you possibly know this feeling of emptiness?

"And for God's sake, don't ask me how I am. What do you expect me to say? That just doesn't make it. Tell me you're sorry, that you're thinking about me. Or better yet, don't say anything. Just hug me. That's enough."

One of my closest friends told me that she sensed people looked at me differently. I felt it, too, as if I had become an object to be pointed out and pitied. I didn't want to be anyone's compassionate flavor of the month. But it was definitely out there. It made me want to travel far away, where no one would know who I was.

In one of the last essays Courtney wrote for class at Michigan, she tried to describe our marriage, and what contrasting personalities George and I are. She called him her "knight in shining armor," and isn't that what all little girls are supposed to say about their daddy?

But she wrote that I was her "best friend . . . and finest enemy." Yes, that's how it was because we were so much alike. It was scary. Courtney and I knew each other inside and out.

Jaime is like her father—cool and detached, analytical,

always keeping score. I love her deeply. But Courtney was my mirror image. Emotional, mercurial. She'd cry over anything but laugh when she caught a tear in my eye. She'd shop all day long and was convinced the best deal was just one store away. One ear to the phone and talking to anyone who picked up at the other end.

She was my comrade, my buddy. Losing her was unbearable in a way that maybe even my husband couldn't understand. In her essay she wrote that I had taken out "a subscription to my diary." But I didn't have to do that. I just knew.

The other bit of advice my friend gave me we followed up on immediately, and it was the best thing we did in those horrible days. We set up a scholarship fund in Courtney's memory.

George and I talked for a while about how we wanted the money to be applied. Finally, we decided that her trip to Israel, when she took the big step and went without knowing anyone else on the trip, was a time of tremendous growth for her. She came back filled with self-assurance and a deeper sense of religious commitment than she had ever shown before.

We felt the best thing we could do in her memory was to give other children the chance to experience a similar trip. So the award would go only to those who agreed to travel outside the auspices of our temple.

In the days after the funeral, when George went back to work and Jaime back to school, the walls started closing in on me. I had taught for ten years before my marriage, and after the kids were a little older I had gone back into the classroom as a substitute. But the thought of teaching again was more than I could handle.

So I stayed home, and every time I walked past her bedroom it was like a dagger in my heart. Her pictures and books and bed and clothes were all right where she had left them. When I could stand it, I started taking some things down and putting them in storage. I was not going to make the room into a shrine.

What I really wanted to do was move, go to a condo or another house, get away from all these memories. But it wasn't just the house. A trip to a mall where we used to shop would start me on a crying jag. The frozen yogurt stand that she loved was off-limits now.

But every time I thought about moving, I couldn't decide what was worse: to stay where we were or to go somewhere with absolutely no touch of our daughter's presence. I was torn every time I entered her room.

Snickers seemed puzzled, too. Courtney's bed had

been his den ever since he was a puppy. He would sleep beneath it every night, and it used to drive Courtney wild when he'd get up on a weekend morning at 7 A.M. and start scratching at her door to be let out.

But now he slept there less and less. Instead, he'd curl up on the floor at the foot of our bed and spend the night there. Occasionally, he'd wander over to his old bed and sleep there for a few hours. But I think he knew something.

About a month after the funeral, we flew to Chicago for a wedding. On the flight over, a friendly young woman seated next to me asked me how many children I had, just the sort of innocent question strangers ask each other. She was flabbergasted when I burst into tears. I couldn't help myself. None of the old answers, even to the most innocuous questions, fit anymore.

I could see what my husband was going through. When he drove up to the condo where I'd been staying in Phoenix, I'd hoped that he would be ready to open up more. It had been the first time we'd been apart since Courtney's death, and he'd had the space to think.

"How was the trip?" I asked him.

"Oh, fine," he said. "Just fine."

One look at his eyes and I knew that it wasn't fine at all. But I didn't know how to tell him that.

So I simply said, "Good. Me, too."

And I held his hand and hoped that we would come through this still together.

CHAPTER 7

———— ✺ ————

Over the years, David Techner has buried several thousand members of his community. What number of them were children he can't recall, although he remembers the pain each one left behind, including ours.

The funeral he can never forget, however, was the one for his own daughter.

"We put Alicia to bed with what the pediatrician thought was the flu," he says, "and she just never woke up. It turned out that she had meningitis. She was eight months old.

"My father-in-law was at the chapel making funeral arrangements with a family who had just lost their twenty-year-old son in a shooting. I had to walk in on them and tell him that his granddaughter was dead. He couldn't go on. I couldn't go on. The family we were talk-ing to was already devastated. There was a snowstorm raging outside. It was like a nightmare.

"I wrote the family a letter of apology later on. They responded that it was the worst day in all of our lives."

That happened in 1978. Since then, David has been able to use his own experience to counsel people who come to him with children to bury.

"The first thing you have to realize is that no one understands the pain you are going through," he says. "People may think they do because they have suffered some kind of loss. But unless you have lost a child, you can't know. And every loss is different. My losing Alicia at eight months is a very different matter than you losing Courtney at eighteen years.

"But there are a few things that are the same, too. The very worst mistake anyone can make, I tell parents, is to believe that the pain will go away eventually. That you're going to 'get over it.' This isn't something that responds to a time frame. This is a lifetime of adjustment.

"A year passes, milestones in your own life go by and you begin to think: 'Why aren't I feeling better? Am I going crazy?' But you can't avoid your child's life. It was real and now it's gone.

"Every so often you think it's in the past, but anything can bring it back. A song you hear on the radio that your child loved. A date on the calendar. With us, the day she died means nothing. But her birthday is murder. High school graduation of the class she would have been in was devastating.

"Friends of mine sometime complain about their kids. They're goofing off at school. Some of them got into drugs. And all the time, I'm thinking to myself, 'You know what, I'd deal with that. Gladly.' It would have been my joy to deal with that.

"Sixteen years after Alicia died I was out signing the papers for a new car, a convertible. The owner of the dealership happened to mention, just in making conversation, that in two years, I could give the keys to my son. Then I remembered that in three more days it would have been Alicia's birthday, and I would have been taking her in to get her driver's license.

"And I just started to cry, sitting right at the man's desk. He looked over at me and he must have thought I was suffering a terrible case of buyer's remorse because he started talking about making some price adjustments. But I just had to sit there and let it out, and it was cleansing.

"I'll tell you something else. As bad as that moment

was, that's how good it felt when I put the top down on that car and drove home. Because, in some way, I had shared that moment with my daughter."

It's not an easy thing to go through life feeling you got cheated, that you were ripped off . . . to know that there is now a place within your heart's deepest core that happiness cannot reach. But that's simply the way it is. Some things must be accepted.

A few days after Courtney's death, I received a letter from a return address I couldn't decipher in a place I didn't know. It turned out that it had been written from a federal prison by former Detroit Tigers pitcher Denny McLain.

When I was a baseball writer in the late 1960s, I had covered Denny's exploits with the Tigers, including the season he won thirty-one games and helped pitch Detroit into the 1968 World Series. Our relationship had always been rather edgy. We were both young, he had a tendency to talk too much, and I had a tendency to put what he said in the newspaper. Sometimes that wasn't the wisest thing to do, but we were both learning.

Later on, his troubles multiplied. He did time in federal prison in Florida and then returned to Detroit after his release. Incredibly, he rebuilt his life doing a morning talk radio show. We also had a bit of a reconciliation. Not that we were ever close friends, but I think his media experience gave him an understanding of my job. He even asked me to pinch hit for him as guest host a few times. I did it, even though it meant rolling out of bed at 4:30 A.M.

But I never could honestly say that I understood Denny. And when he threw it all away again—becoming involved in a pension fund blowout scam that devastated the retirees of a small meat-packing company and ending up back in prison—I was completely baffled. What can drive a man to do that with his life?

In the midst of his radio career, however, his daughter had been killed in an automobile accident. After that, Denny seemed to go to pieces again, making unreasonable demands on his station and plunging into this other thing.

I think now that there had to be a connection. Sure, he had been in trouble before, but I know it doesn't take much to push someone inclined to mischief to stray from the right path. The death of a child is more than a push; it is a hurricane.

But McLain's letter irritated me. His message, repeated several times, was: "The pain never goes away."

I didn't want to hear that in the days after Courtney's death. I still chose to believe that I could make it all right again. But of all the things said to me in those days, Denny's words were the most honest.

His career was in a shambles for the second time. He had just been divorced from his wife of more than thirty years. He was in prison, for God's sake. Yet the greatest pain was still the loss of his daughter, and I understood completely.

Dave Techner had one other bit of advice, involving marriage and the strain that such a death places on it. After the death of a child, almost three out of four marriages end within a few years. Whether other factors are involved, whether the marriage was going down the tubes anyhow, the stats don't reveal. But the strain, as Sherry and I were learning, was very real.

"We became afraid of each other," says David of his own marriage. "We were both lost in our own grief and were scared that if we tried to reach out to the other that they wouldn't be in the same place.

"A psychiatrist told me that what we had to do was

turn off the TV, disconnect the phone, and for fifteen minutes, seven days a week, set aside time to talk. Talk about anything and everything. If it was about Alicia, that was good. Or it could be the weather, work, anything. We just had to start talking.

"The process is extremely difficult for a Type-A personality, someone who is used to getting things done, someone who is accustomed to solving problems. But the death of his child, the thing that he held most dear, he was powerless to stop. This is one problem he can't fix, and it just eats away at him. These are the people who have the toughest time, and whose marriages are most at risk.

"But you know what? In our case, it turned out that when we started talking, we rediscovered how much we genuinely liked each other. In a very definite way, this strengthened our marriage."

When I met Sherry in Arizona we hadn't come to that place yet. Not even close.

CHAPTER 8

———cᴧꜱ———

We still had no answers, and that was a big part of the problem. We had no idea how Courtney could have fallen through that window.

A car crash or an illness we could understand: terrible things, but comprehensible just the same. Falling through a window made no sense.

The university told us it had inspected the window in her room to see if the restraint that kept it from opening wider than twelve inches was broken. Housing officials claimed it was working—although investigation showed that the restraints on one out of every six windows at Markley, by the university's own admission, were broken.

Sherry's brother, Barry Bershad, and her cousin, Stan Bershad, had volunteered to go to the room at Markley

Hall the day after the funeral to clean it out and bring home Courtney's things. Barry took me aside when he returned.

"There's no way she goes through that window," he told me. "Nothing was touched on the window ledge. There was no sign of anything outside. I can't understand it."

So when the phone call came a few weeks later, I was probably already half prepared in my mind. The call came to my office, from an older man with an accent, possibly Eastern European.

"Mr. Cantor, I have information on how your daughter died," he said. "Would you please meet with me?"

He wouldn't give me his name or say anything more over the phone, so we arranged to meet in two days at a Denny's restaurant in a Detroit suburb. I called an attorney friend to see what I should do. He told me to take someone with me to the meeting, to have him wait outside in the parking lot, and when the informant showed up to take down the plate number on the car. Then my friend would check the identification.

Barry was up for this cloak-and-dagger operation. We arrived at Denny's early, staked out a table by a window, and waited.

Our man showed up driving an older car, and he walked with a pronounced limp. We were sure it was the guy. He just looked like someone who would arrange a mysterious rendezvous at a Denny's. We scribbled down the plate number from where we sat, and I walked to the door to meet him.

"Not here," he said when he saw our table. "Too open." Instead, he walked to the farthest corner in the back of the restaurant and lowered himself slowly into the seat.

"Is he a cop?" he asked, his eyes darting toward Barry. Reassured that Barry was not a policeman, our mystery guest said, "I don't want this taped. What I'm going to tell you cannot be heard by the wrong people." He stared at his hands for a few seconds and then began.

"Mr. Cantor," he said, "I have reason to believe your daughter's death was no accident. I think she was murdered by a group with ties to the neo-Nazis and the Ku Klux Klan. They are targeting the children of prominent Jews."

This news was staggering and I suppose my face revealed that.

"I see you are skeptical," said our informant. "That is only natural. But I have the proof."

So for the next half hour we sat there while this guy spun out the most convoluted conspiracy theory of all time, tying Courtney's death to every other spectacular unsolved crime in recent history.

If I had been up on my Internet research, I wouldn't have been so surprised. I found out later about a web page where such crackpots could find each other. His premise was that because I had written some columns critical of President Clinton, Courtney was killed by operatives from Clinton's administration who were trying to silence me.

A few dozen people actually discussed this scenario online, as if it were sane.

The man at Denny's finally reached the coda of his composition.

"When was your daughter's birthday?" he asked.

November 11, I told him. His eyes widened.

"Of course," he murmured. "Stupid. How could I have missed it? Don't you see? It's all so clear now.

"November 11. Eleven-Eleven. What is the eleventh letter of the alphabet? It's K. Eleven-Eleven. KK. One letter short of KKK—Ku Klux Klan. And add another 11 to your daughter's birth date and what do you have?

November 22. And what happened on a November 22? John F. Kennedy was shot."

He raised both his hands as if any idiot could now see the connection, and I had to admit that it was all pretty astounding.

"But I have a question," I said, the first one I had asked. "If someone came into the room and threw Courtney through that window, wouldn't there have been signs of a struggle? But nothing on the window ledge had been disturbed."

The man fixed me with a stare for a long moment.

"You're very good," he said finally. "That is an excellent point. I will have to consult with my associates before I can answer it."

That seemed to end the interview. We walked to the door, and my informant promised to be back in touch with me. I told him that I would wait in keen anticipation.

When he was gone, Barry took out the paper on which he had written the license number and tore it up. Just to cap things off, when Barry returned to his car he found that he had a flat tire.

Coincidence? We didn't think so.

—⚬—

As ludicrous as this encounter may have been, Ann Arbor police took several weeks before officially removing homicide as a possible cause of Courtney's death.

On the Michigan campus, however, many students had come to their own conclusion. Many people believed that she had taken her own life.

Mercifully, Sherry and I did not become aware of this rumor until several months afterward. But several of Courtney's closest friends heard the talk and were outraged.

"The stupid thing about those rumors is that I'd never seen her so happy," said Bekah Parker, one of her tightest buddies since the sixth grade. "My dad and I had dinner with Courtney the night she died and she was bubbling. Everything was working out the way she wanted it.

"She got into the sorority she wanted. She was confident that she was going to be fine academically. Her roommate was great. It was all coming together for her."

But the gossip was understandable. The students were as puzzled as we were. They knew the setup of the windows in Markley and could not imagine how anyone could fall through them, unless it was a deliberate act.

Besides, so many people already knew someone who had committed suicide. It is a national plague. With all the publicity given to teenage gun deaths, the 2000 National Vital Statistics Report of the U.S. Department of Health and Human Services revealed that 54 percent of them were self-inflicted.

Occasionally, a cluster of suicides will take place, because the act is highly susceptible to imitation. That happened in Plano, Texas, in the mid-1990s, and a spate of news stories was written about it then.

Sometimes a highly visible celebrity decides to make an end. When rock musician Kurt Cobain killed himself, culture watchers interpreted the act as a reflection of the pervasive sense of nihilism and despair that drew young people to his work. In early 1997, five male students at Michigan State University took their own lives within a four-month span.

But studies indicate that it is not classroom pressures that lead to campus suicides as much as the removal of a familiar support system. Courtney was surrounded by friends, and just forty-five minutes from a loving home.

Such high-profile cases prompt the standard media

commentaries on adolescent anxiety and the lack of adult comprehension. Then the phenomenon goes subterranean again until the next breakout.

In virtually every case of suicide, however, the act is accompanied by unmistakable signs of prolonged depression or by threats overtly stated to friends. Even the most upbeat personalities undergo a noticeable change in the weeks before such a death occurs. Almost always some warning has been sounded.

But parents are understandably unwilling to accept such an explanation. When a child dies under ambiguous circumstances, they search for other answers. I am sure the woman who came by our house to drop off the booklet she had written after her own daughter's suicide felt she was comforting us. When we failed to respond, I'm sure she thought we were simply in denial.

The best thing I can do is let Courtney speak for herself. Two months after her death, university investigators brought me a paper they had found on her desk in the dormitory room. It was a two-page handwritten essay, her last class assignment.

Before giving it to me, they had turned it over to psychologists to see if it contained any possible hint of a suicide profile. Unsurprisingly, they said it didn't.

Courtney wrote about the end of the sorority rush period and her reaction to the experience:

The process of rush is finally over!! . . . At the end of my last paper I talked about the struggle I was going through in picking a sorority house. In the past week I have made my decision and am now a member of Chi Omega.

I am very happy with my decision for many reasons. The first reason is because this decision was made independently from most of my friends. While many of my friends chose to follow one another into the same house, I chose independence. In the end, I had to do what was right for me and what would make me happy.

Because of my decision I don't have the comfort that many of them have because they know almost everyone in their house. I am meeting mostly new faces, many of whom don't live in my dorm. Therefore, perhaps it is a little more difficult for me to adjust. However, I am excited to meet all these new people and to find friends I ordinarily would never meet. I took a risk when I chose this house because of its diversity. I am proud of myself for following my own heart. . . .

I know that I have a lot of fun to look forward to in

my next 4 years of college. But one thing I have learned through this entire process is that we live in a very harsh environment with extremely judgmental people. A few of my friends did not get into a sorority at all and this is not because they are not wonderful people. Rather it's because somebody decided they didn't like them. I think it's sad and unfortunate that the sorority system functions in a way that great people are overlooked.

If that is the work of a person bent on self-destruction, then I'm Napoleon.

But a larger question had begun insinuating itself into my thoughts. What can the university be thinking of in sanctioning the exhausting and tension-filled Greek rush period just weeks after the freshman class arrives on campus to begin life in a totally new environment?

I had to learn the immediate facts surrounding Courtney's death. But clearly I also had many unanswered questions about its context.

CHAPTER 9

———⚬⚬———

I didn't write a single word of the first front-page byline I ever received.

In a suburban homicide, a middle-aged woman was found strangled in her bathtub. As the youngest reporter working the Sunday shift, I was sent out to obtain a photograph of the woman. I was not supposed to do any actual reporting.

But while I was out there, the cops broke the case. The teenaged kid next door had done it, and my job was to go to the home of his parents and ask their reaction to having their son charged with murder.

Steeling myself to this assignment, I talked my way inside and conducted an emotional interview. I then called Cap'n Ralph, the night rewrite man, and gave him my notes. "Cap'n Ralph" was not an affectionate nickname. He was called that because his personality resembled that of the boss on a Southern chain gang. Cap'n Ralph, cigarette dangling from his fingers and eyes squinting in perpetual anger, was acknowledged to be the meanest man in North America.

He hated everyone, especially people who phoned the city desk to pester him with their problems after the bars closed. On one occasion, he shut down a teary caller by saying, "Buddy, my advice to you is just start heading down Third Street towards the river, and keep walking until your hat floats." A compassionate man was the Cap'n.

But he reserved his special venom for young reporters, whom he regarded as both unworthy scum and a pack of boobs. So when I called in my notes, he grimly began peppering me with more questions. When I couldn't respond to his satisfaction, he sent me back into the house for the answers. He did this three times, and my humiliation grew deeper every time I had to knock on the door again. In the end, however, I learned to get it right the first time. The next morning, although the prose was that of Cap'n Ralph, the byline was mine.

So I understood the routine when the media mob

descended on us after Courtney's death. I'd been there, and I sympathized with the reporters. I knew any number of places they would rather have been.

The situation did place me in an odd position. I was a fairly prominent member of the *Detroit News,* and here were our hated rivals at the *Free Press* on the phone asking me questions. I felt the circumstances transcended competition, so I respected their aggressive approach and did my best to make myself available and cooperative. I even answered one phone call while sitting in Dave Techner's office selecting Courtney's coffin.

I don't know how many interviews I gave those first few days, but I could see that both the print and broadcast media already had the story pegged. It was to be another instance of Binge Drinking on Campus.

None of the medical examiner's findings had been made available. No evidence was released about the window in her room. All the details of the death were sketchy. But the media had made up its mind, and nothing was going to change it.

In my thirty-eight years as a journalist, I have watched in dismay as my profession has plummeted in public credibility to somewhere between that of used car sales and television evangelism. Bias and stupidity are the foremost reasons to blame for this. But one of the biggest reasons for public disdain is the media's insistence on categorizing a story immediately—jumping to a conclusion, then reporting on that basis no matter what the facts may show.

The process is much of the problem. Assigning editors who never leave the office direct on-the-scene reporters to find facts that support a preconceived outline. The news becomes scripted, and the budget line on which the story is sold at the daily news meeting drives the coverage. Anything that raises questions about the preconceived scenario is ignored.

To make it worse, the angles that editors seize upon are often pop-culture clichés. Home Alone for every story involving a child who comes to harm with no adult in the house. Field of Dreams for every amateur who aspires to athletic glory. The slain gang member who was "just getting his life turned around." Every death a "tragedy" and every life spared a "miracle." Now Binge Drinking had become the angle du jour.

Life is more complex than that, but sometimes I wonder if journalism's essential mission hasn't been reduced to belaboring the obvious.

So I understood what was happening now that I was on the receiving end. As a journalist, I was dismayed. As a parent, I was furious.

In my first column after my daughter's death, I said that I did not want Courtney to "become the poster child for the campaign against campus drinking." Although the cause is excellent, I was not at all convinced that story applied in this case. Too many other factors were yet to be explained.

I told friends that I was not surprised Courtney had been drinking. But I would be flabbergasted if it turned out she was drunk.

Only the most naive parents can possibly believe that their children will go through high school without experimenting once or twice with alcohol or pot. The crucial factors are these: Is there a pattern of use? Is it affecting their grades or personality?

Neither factor was in evidence with Courtney. She was in the National Honor Society, played junior varsity tennis and softball, was on the school forensics team, volunteered for community service, worked at a variety of jobs. Her mood swings were small and easily righted, just the normal stuff of adolescence.

We readily gave her permission to go on the senior trip to Cancún with her friends simply because we knew no pattern of substance abuse existed. She had earned our trust.

She came back with all sorts of junk from a place called Señor Frog, and I assumed more was going on there than Kermit had ever imagined. But when we sent her off to the University of Michigan, Sherry and I were sure in our minds that our daughter had no drinking problem.

The medical examiner's report came back indicating that Courtney had a blood alcohol level of 0.059—well below intoxication. If she had been behind the wheel of a car, for example, there would have been no citation given for driving under the influence.

Many news stories immediately speculated, nonetheless, that because of her small stature, a reading of 0.059 would have a greater effect on her than on a bigger person. But that number reflects a constant ratio based on a fixed volume. The speculation was like saying the IQ of a large person should be measured differently than that of a smaller person because the head is bigger.

Evidence shows that it does take fewer drinks for a small-statured woman to reach that blood alcohol level, but that proposition is entirely different. Newspaper reporters are notoriously inaccurate in analyzing statistics, however, because most of them have the math skills of a watermelon.

So the facts still didn't add up. Something else had to be going on here.

Only one reporter, Suzanne Wangler, at the NBC affiliate in Detroit, called me to ask about the safety of the windows in her dorm. That angle seemed obvious, and I told her so. But after one day she was pulled off the story, and the focus returned to Binge Drinking again.

48 Hours urgently wanted to do the Binge Drinking story. A rash of alcohol-related campus deaths had occurred in Michigan. A survey taken in 1999 showed that Michigan State University also had the second-highest rate of alcohol-related arrests in the country.

Most of these incidents involved binge drinking, which is the practice of deliberately setting out to consume as much alcohol as possible in a short time period with the sole intent of getting drunk. That activity was the news peg in these stories, the element that supposedly separated the campus drinking of today from the innocent, madcap boozing of the past.

As a point of fact, a study from the Harvard School of

Public Health found that binge drinking, as opposed to overall alcohol consumption, actually had declined somewhat from a peak incidence in 1993. That study was released one month before Courtney's death.

An underlying theme was that something in the state's culture—the legacy of Michigan's auto-worker, blue-collar mindset—contributed to an atmosphere in which excessive drinking was condoned. That opinion, too, is not borne out by statistical evidence. Alcohol consumption in Michigan is lower on a per capita basis than in California, Nevada, and several states in the Northeast. But don't try to argue with the media when it builds up a head of steam.

Even though I was uneasy with the premise, I agreed to the *48 Hours* interview, which was set for early January. A tabloid TV show called at about the same time, but I turned it down. *48 Hours* was CBS. I trusted the brand name.

Police reports indicated that Courtney had been drinking some champagne at the party, but spent most of the night throwing up in the frat house bathroom. Now that sounded like Courtney. Before she ever drank enough to binge, she would have become sick to her stomach.

Nonetheless, a few months later, the *Free Press* did a front-page story on binge drinking, and my daughter's name appeared in the lead paragraph as example number one. I was disgusted. No credible evidence ever indicated that binge drinking was a factor in her death.

I had learned the newspaper business at the *Free Press*. That's where Cap'n Ralph taught me to get the facts right the first time. Even though I had left the paper many years before, I still had a lingering regard for it. This story staggered me. I now understood the attitude of all those people who ever complained that they had been mugged in print.

The real story wouldn't start to come together for several weeks. But I was more concerned now with trying to hold my family together, as well as myself.

CHAPTER 10

———— ↺ ————

If anyone had suggested that Sherry and I join a bereavement support group, I would have run full-tilt in the opposite direction. The last thing I wanted to do was sit around a room sharing intimacies with a bunch of strangers.

I did not require any psychologist to instruct me on how to grieve. An adult who encounters the inevitable storms of life should not need a weatherman to know which way the wind blows.

Or so I thought.

What rescued us from despair was a renewal of our religious faith and the recognition that without it our grief would have no boundary. To my astonishment, the instrument of our healing was a support group, only disguised under another name.

Minyan. The Jewish daily worship service at which mourners gather to recite the memorial prayer. A support group established centuries before anyone had thought to use that name.

I was not an especially observant person. My clearest memory of religious school was contriving to miss the bus that took me there. On a few occasions I boarded the bus and got to school, only to immediately walk home, complaining of any number of ailments from sore throat to rapture of the deep. My mother was convinced she was raising the sickest kid in the neighborhood, although she was always heartened by my miraculous recoveries just in time for a ballgame or the weekend.

Eventually, I caught on that if I just showed up two days a week for bar mitzvah lessons, everyone would be happy. The teachers were overjoyed to see me go when I turned thirteen, and further instruction was never considered.

I was raised in the Conservative tradition. While we kept kosher and always walked to services on the High

Holidays, we rarely attended on the Sabbath, nor were my parents active in synagogue functions.

That level of observance suited me fine. When I was in college, I succumbed to the temptation of pork and shrimp and figured that I was by then a lost soul.

Sherry grew up at a Reform temple, and with no hesitation I became a member there after our marriage. Temple Israel was in the process of growing into one of the largest congregations in North America. Not coincidentally, Temple Israel was also introducing more traditional practices into its worship: expanded use of Hebrew prayer, encouraging the use of a skullcap, a ritual bath.

Such practices would be repelled at many temples. The American Reform movement had grown up in the late nineteenth century as a rejection of supposedly outmoded and empty ceremonial observance. But many younger people now felt comfort reconnecting with an older tradition, desiring a religion that demanded more of them and emphasized what was required instead of what could be discarded. Temple Israel began to answer that need and thrived as a result.

Among the traditions it restored was a morning service, the minyan. The word refers to the minimum of ten adults who must be present for the most important prayers, including Kaddish, the memorial prayer, to be said. Judaism emphasizes prayer as a communal activity. I would soon understand why.

When a close relative dies, members of the family are directed to say Kaddish for eleven months. Why eleven? According to the sages, if the prayers are scrupulously recited, even the worst of people will be with God in a year. Since you wouldn't want to classify your relative as among the worst of people, you stop at eleven months.

Despite having fallen away from the traditions of my youth, I knew beyond question that I would say the prayers for my daughter. What I didn't know was what saying the prayers would do for me.

Minyan was held in the temple library at a long, rectangular table set up in a central space amid the shelves. About twenty chairs were placed around it.

When I first walked in, exactly one week after Courtney's funeral, I didn't know a single person sitting there, but they knew me. They appeared to be expecting my arrival.

"How goodly are your tents, O Jacob; your habitations, O Israel."

The opening words to the morning service were sung in Hebrew and then recited in English. We went around the table, each person reading a paragraph or two of the English text. Minyan here was entirely a lay service, with no clergy present.

Some of the prayers were familiar and others were not. But when I wasn't missing the bus or faking a stomach ailment, I had managed to pick up a rudimentary knowledge of Hebrew. I followed the prayers easily. The service was not going to be difficult.

The final prayer was Kaddish, and before it was recited we again went around the table. Each person said the name of the one being remembered.

"When we say Kaddish today," said Solly, who led the service, "we will all be remembering Courtney."

In the Conservative tradition, the practice is that only people who are grieving recite the prayer. Others join in only for the congregational responses. I suspect part of this approach is superstitious dread—that reciting Kaddish when your parents or other close relatives are still living might give the Angel of Death some ideas.

So while I was familiar with the words of Kaddish, this was the first time I had actually said them out loud in the temple. The experience rocked me, and I stumbled over the opening lines. But soon I found myself caught up in the prayer's momentum, and its familiar rhythms carried me through to the end.

Then we had bagels and coffee, and everybody went home. The whole thing was done in about forty-five minutes. It would be the pattern of my mornings for the next eleven months.

I am not good with names and faces. As a journalist, I can interview someone intensively for thirty minutes, and if I met them on the street the next day I'd have no idea who they were. My wife, on the other hand, can sit at a table at a wedding reception with someone, not see them again for twenty years, and recognize them immediately when she encounters them once more. This difference baffles me and annoys my wife, who feels I am being stupid on purpose.

So I took a while to sort out the minyan group.

Solly, the leader on that first day, he had flown planes

over The Hump into China during World War II and always showed up half an hour before everyone else to make sure the prayer books were distributed with military precision.

Carolyn, who said she had gone to high school with me (my usual blank on the face), and her sister Nancy called themselves the Spice Girls.

Ben and Sam were in their eighties. Each had lost his wife a few weeks apart. Although they belonged to different synagogues, they had been separately advised by friends to attend this service. They hadn't known each other before but discovered they lived in the same apartment complex and began driving together every morning. When one couldn't come for one reason or another, the other one fretted. Minyan provided what was now missing in their lives: someone to worry about.

Estelle's hobby was doing stand-up comedy at homes for the aged. When she started doing these routines, she had told the director of one of the homes that she didn't know how far she could go with it because she only knew nine or ten real good jokes.

"Don't worry about it," he had told her. "By the time you come back, they'll have forgotten them all."

I had known Norm as the father of one of Courtney's friends. Kenny was a rotund man of about fifty with the likable demeanor of a natural salesman. I learned later that he owned a successful insurance agency, which did not surprise me. Dr. Marc was a dentist whose wife had just lost a long, courageous struggle with a debilitating lung disease.

Ted had won an Oscar for his short cartoon, *Crunch Bird*. Batya had experienced a religious awakening a few years before, changed her English name to a Hebrew one, and began a serious study of Judaism. She always led the service on Tuesday morning, and on that day many women would attend for the sole purpose of hearing Batya's lesson from that week's Bible text. They drew inspiration from her.

Sid and Henrietta were mourning the death of their daughter, too. She had been my age when she died, a woman in her late fifties, but that did not make their loss any easier to bear than ours. Henrietta wept each day when she mentioned her daughter's name before saying Kaddish.

Coming to minyan meant getting out of bed at about 6:30, a good hour and a half before my job demanded. I have never been an enthusiastic or even especially coherent person in the mornings. It is usually all I can do to breathe and swallow at that hour. I was not glad at the prospect of arising before dawn for most of the year and making my way to the temple for prayers.

After a few weeks, however, I discovered something. I was looking forward to starting my day this way. I felt a calm there, a warmth that lasted through the morning. I urged Sherry to attend, too. She thought it would be too difficult for her, but after some discussion she agreed.

Soon we were arriving a little bit earlier, to sip coffee and talk. We had become so weary of explaining our emotions, of discussing with well-meaning friends where we were in our minds. At minyan, everyone understood. Emotions were always close to the surface with no need to apologize or explain. Everyone was there for the same reason.

We were comforted participating in a religious observance that stretched back across the centuries. We recited the same words that had been said by ancestors whose existence has been forgotten. But the prayers lived on, timeless, consoling. We had walked into a room full of strangers and found another family, bound by grief if not blood. As the worst sorrow began to ease, we found that these ties remained. We stayed on with the minyan group, as did many of the others, long after the eleven months were up.

We looked out for each other's needs. Jeff had lost his sister and could not read aloud without breaking down at certain emotional parts of the service. We all made sure that if his turn came at that point someone else would unobtrusively pick up the reading. When special prayers for the ailing were recited, we said them not only for our own but mentioned the family of the others in the group.

On Friday morning there was no minyan. Instead, we attended the evening Sabbath service and recited Kaddish there. Temple Israel is so large it holds two services on Friday nights. One is a formal gathering in the main sanctuary, where the bar mitzvah and bat mitzvah services are held.

The other is an informal service in the social hall. People dress casually, sit in folding chairs, and hear a shorter sermon. There is no reading from the Torah. On many Fridays that service is the better attended of the two, and in the summer months the service is packed when it is held under the sky in the Temple garden.

People who attend minyan are only a tiny percentage of the temple's membership. So before Friday services began, our group would seek each other out for a special greeting, a kiss, a handshake, as if within the congregation we were members of a special society who carried a mark that set us apart.

When my children lived at home, attending Friday services wouldn't even have occurred to us. We made no effort to sit down together for a Sabbath meal and rarely lit candles to mark the start of the day of rest.

On one occasion, Sherry invited some friends who weren't Jewish to come over for Friday dinner, and in a fit of religious inspiration she asked me to give the kids a Sabbath blessing. No such request had ever been made of me before, and for a terrible moment I didn't know what to say. Fortunately, I remembered the lyrics to one of the songs from *Fiddler on the Roof* and used them. That improvisation seemed to please everyone, and I'm sure our friends went home feeling they had been part of a warm weekly ritual.

But now if we missed a Friday we felt diminished. This service, too, with its comforting songs and its sense of belonging to a tradition that stretched back unbroken through the millennia, had folded us within its embrace.

Norm not only attended daily minyan and Friday services, but he felt compelled to do more. He put in long days as a financial adviser and, like us, had never before felt a need to come to these services. But when both his parents died within a year of each other, he became a regular.

Dissatisfied because there was a separate prayer book for people who could not read Hebrew, Norm bought software in that language. He then rewrote the minyan books on his computer so that they could be combined into one. He also began study to lead the prayer services in homes during the period of *shiva,* when the Kaddish was recited there instead of in the temple.

Once or twice a week, after a full day at the office, Norm would receive a call to attend a house of mourning to lead one of these services. They became a welcome part of the pattern of his life. Minyan had changed him, too.

We decided that seeing these people only at services wasn't enough. Now they were numbered among our closest friends.

So we arranged informal dinner get-togethers with the Spice Girls and Dr. Marc, and another with Norm and

Kenny, meeting for an evening out about once a month.

"I have now heard everything," one of the rabbis said when he learned about this. "From minyan to dinner clubs."

But the need for the comfort we had gained from one another did not end with the final "amen." Sherry and I had changed from the people we were before Courtney died. An entirely new door had opened for us both.

CHAPTER 11

———∽———

Even with minyan for support, though, other doors remained shut. For Sherry and me, communication was still difficult and in some areas had closed down altogether.

I chose not to talk much about Courtney because I felt that it was too distressing for my wife. These discussions quickly led to tears, and I felt that my job was to move us past the tears. That's what a man is supposed to do, so I steered our conversations away from Courtney.

But our daughter's death was, of course, the first thing on our minds when we woke up in the morning and the last thing at night. Her passing crowded out almost every other thought. It was the fire-breathing dragon sitting in our living room that we both refused to acknowledge. If we didn't talk about it, maybe it would go away.

When I visited the cemetery for the first time, I went by myself. It was a drizzly December day, about six weeks after the funeral.

According to Jewish tradition, one only visits a grave on the anniversary of the death and between the High Holidays. This is one tradition that I felt could be discarded. I wasn't about to stay away from my daughter's grave for a year.

I knew the cemetery well. The grandmother for whom Courtney was named rests there, and so does her husband, my grandfather, for whom I am named. Various uncles, aunts, and cousins are there, as are Sherry's parents and grandparents.

When asked how a nomadic people can lay claim to any specific piece of land, one of the great Native American leaders replied, "Our lands are where our dead lie buried."

Modern Americans aren't quite as restless as the Plains Indians of the mid-nineteenth century. But we do move around a lot, and so the same question arises: Where is home? The old answer still serves. Our families had staked their claim to this corner of the world through our dead that lay beyond the cemetery gates.

Courtney's grave was, at first, hard to find. The area where we had bought our plot looked much different than it did on the day we buried her. No green carpet leading from the curb to the gravesite. No open cavity to receive the coffin. We hadn't put up a stone yet. All that guided me to it was a small white marker with her name and date of death on it.

I had shoveled the first two scoops of dirt upon the coffin after the burial service—another old tradition. Then I had walked over to where my cousin, Jeff Shillman, was standing. We had done everything together as kids: gone to ballgames, rode our bikes all over the neighborhood, made each other laugh on long summer vacation days.

We had often told each other, long before Courtney died, that the worst thing that could possibly happen to anyone was to lose a child. Now he put his arms around me.

"Why did life have to get so goddamn hard?" he said.

I had written a column twelve years before about how I still didn't feel like a grown-up, that adulthood was just an elaborate charade. We are only kids pretending to be doctors, lawyers, and writers, and when the real adults found out what we were up to we'd be in big trouble.

But now every bit of me felt like a grown-up. I didn't think I would ever feel like a child again.

I had always loved to teach Courtney things: the words to old songs, history, favorite poems.

But in death she had gone beyond my capacity to teach. She now knew far more than I. She knew the answer to the greatest puzzle of all.

When I drove up to the cemetery I had felt an eager anticipation, as if I were actually going to see my daughter again. But there was only the little white marker and the wind and the silent raindrops. I stood there for a few solitary moments, found a pebble, placed it on the grass beside the marker, and drove away.

I didn't tell Sherry I had gone. I knew it would lead to tears, and my job was to get us past that.

But a few weeks later she asked when we would make our first trip to the cemetery. I told her then that I already had done it. She seemed a little surprised but didn't mention it again.

After her next visit to her psychiatrist, Sherry asked

me to go for a session with the doctor, too. I had never done such a thing before, and I was not especially eager to do it now. I was, in fact, deeply uncomfortable with the idea.

But she had asked, and I had promised to get us through this. If "getting us through this" meant seeing a psychiatrist, then I was up for it.

As it turned out, that promise was the problem. Sherry had been deeply hurt by my decision to spare her emotions and visit the cemetery alone.

It didn't take the doctor long to get to the point.

"What makes you think that you have to carry this burden by yourself?" she asked.

I was genuinely puzzled. *That was my role, my responsibility as a man, as a loving husband and father. How could I do otherwise?*

"A man has got to be strong," I protested.

"How do you know that?" she asked.

"That's what my father is," I said. "My father is strong."

My dad's strength had been tempered by the Great Depression. He had to drop out of college, on a track that would have led him to medical school, to support his family when my grandfather lost his business and had a heart attack. Instead of studying anatomy, at the age of nineteen my dad was throwing beef carcasses around a freezing slaughterhouse.

But he got through that. Years later, just before his previous college credits would have expired, he went through night school at Wayne University while driving a city bus during the day. He earned a degree in accounting and so impressed the head of the school's department that he recommended my dad for a job with one of the big national firms. But they weren't in the market for hiring any Jews in the late 1940s. He started work, instead, for a much lower salary at a small local firm.

He made it through that, too, and worked his way up to a partnership in one of Detroit's leading accounting firms. Then he discovered that his partner was quietly going through a mental breakdown and had skimmed funds from their clients' advances.

Legally, my dad could have escaped liability. But he never considered that option. At enormous financial sacrifice, he repaid every dime, because it was the right thing to do.

I loved my father and was proud to be his son. I had

always hoped that when my time of testing came, I could measure up to him. Well, this was it, and I was trying my damndest.

"But nobody asked you to do that," repeated the doctor. "Don't you know that Sherry needs to help you, too?"

That didn't make sense at first. I would have bridled had anyone suggested that my attitudes were sexist. I was the father of daughters and had wanted every opportunity for them. I always encouraged them to believe that they could accomplish anything, could compete as equals with anyone.

But I never thought that women who wanted to be equal also had to be strong. Sherry needed to be pulled through this, yes, but she needed to pull me through it, too. Instead, I was refusing to be rescued, pushing her away.

I didn't have to carry the weight alone. It was crushing both of us.

A few days later, a package arrived from Israel. I recognized the name on the return address. It was from one of the counselors on the trip Courtney had taken two years before. Jean-Claude, the cute one from France over whom all the girls had swooned.

He had sent a short note expressing his sorrow at learning of Courtney's death. While looking through some material from that summer, he wrote, he had come across a photograph of her. He had taken the liberty of having it blown up and sent to us because it expressed her contribution to the trip so well.

She was squatting in front of a piece of blue canvas, maybe a downed tent. She was in shorts and hiking boots. But it was her face, nose crinkled up in laughter, eyes dancing, that had captured her. I had seen that expression hundreds of times as we shared a joke. It truly had distilled in one photograph who she was.

As Sherry and I looked at the picture on our kitchen table, I started to cry.

All the grief that had been stored inside me came pouring out in that instant, released for the first time. No guarded emotions anymore. I sobbed endlessly, all the anger and the loss finally unbottled.

My wife sat beside me, her arms tight around me, crying softly, giving me comfort. Sharing the weight.

CHAPTER 12

———⌁———

No one can remember now who first dreamed up their nickname. The Chit-Chats. Maybe a teacher, maybe one of the many guys who had met with their displeasure. But it fit, and it followed the six of them all through high school.

They all talked a mile a minute and incessantly, too. At lunch, in the halls, in class. A raging flood of words. They would have been their teachers' despair if it hadn't been for the fact that they were all straight-A students. They were just a trifle garrulous.

Jen Raznick and Karen Estrine, Bekah Parker and Nicole Siegel, Rachel Zlotoff and Courtney.

From middle school through senior prom, they were

each other's best friends. Fiercely loyal, protective, and cohesive. At an age when most teenaged girls are at each other's throats or plunging daggers of gossip into their friends' backs, the Chit-Chats stood apart. When they all turned sixteen, they went to a photo studio and posed for pictures, which were then mounted as tiny plastic cutouts. It was their mutual Sweet Sixteen gift to each other.

As hard as Courtney's death hit Sherry, Jaime, and me, it was devastating to these friends. Death was not supposed to happen, not to them. Their lives rested upon bright, unfailing promise, buoyed by high expectations. People warned you about this sort of thing in those stupid lectures on safety and substance abuse that nobody paid any attention to, because they applied to other kids in other schools.

Andover High is consistently ranked among the top public secondary schools in America. It was the specific reason Sherry and I bought a house where we did. We wanted Andover for our daughters.

The school has a tough, competitive atmosphere, although many of the students had a little more cash to spend in their pockets and drove flashier cars than we would have liked. Some kids wilt under the academic and social pressure and choose another school, or throw up their hands, give up, and coast. Jaime didn't have an especially happy time at Andover, although her marks qualified her for Michigan.

But the Chit-Chats thrived because they had each other. Nicole and Bekah wound up going to Ann Arbor with Courtney. Jen and Karen headed to Emory, and Rachel to Tufts.

They all swore they would keep in touch all through life, stand up at each others' weddings. These friendships were forever. No one thought forever would come so soon.

They were five of the six pallbearers at Courtney's funeral.

"When I answered the phone in Atlanta and both my parents were on the line, I knew something bad had happened," says Jen. "When they told me, it still didn't seem real. It was like I was hearing about a stranger. Then I ran outside my dorm and tried to find Karen."

"When Jen came up to me in the school cafeteria, she looked frantic," Karen recalls. "I took her hand and she walked me to the far side of the room. Then she said,

'Courtney Cantor died.' I remember she emphasized each word and used both her first and last name, as if she was trying to tell me that this is real, it's our Courtney.

"We held each other and just cried and sobbed. My friends came running up to us and we couldn't talk. All Jen kept saying was, 'Our friend died. She was our friend.'"

The two of them managed to track down Rachel in Massachusetts to tell her, and all three were instructed by their parents to fly home immediately.

Nicole had pledged the same sorority as Courtney and had seen her at the party.

"She didn't look like she was drunk or anything," she said. "She was dancing, having a good time. She was just acting like Courtney. Afterwards, I kept on telling myself, 'You shouldn't have left her. You should have stayed with her.' But the more I thought about it as the weeks went by, the more I was convinced that there was just no sign of trouble. I couldn't possibly have known anything was wrong."

A little more than a year before this, Nicole was sleeping over at our house when the phone rang in the middle of the night. It was Shelly, her mother, telling us that Nicole's father had died of a heart attack in Arizona.

Courtney had watched her friend dissolve in grief at the loss. After Nicole was driven home, our daughter crawled into bed with Sherry and me, as she used to as an infant. She wouldn't stop clinging to me until morning. I often think about that night, and how it should have been me clinging to her.

Nicole and Bekah were also living in Markley, and on the morning of the accident they were called with all the other residents to the dorm reception area. All they were told was that someone had fallen and was injured. They looked everywhere for Courtney but didn't see her and began expecting the worst.

Shortly after 10 A.M., after the university had managed to contact Jaime and me, the announcement was made to the dorm residents that Courtney was dead.

"My first thought was, 'My God, I've just heard something so terrible that I've got to go and tell Courtney,'" said Bekah. "It was a total disconnect. All I knew is that we had shared everything, every bit of news for so many years. I had to do a mental double-take to realize that this was something I couldn't tell her."

Both Nicole and Bekah spoke at a memorial service for Courtney on the Diag, the day after the funeral. A few hundred students carrying candles in the autumn darkness walked from Markley to this traditional campus gathering place for words of remembrance.

Her two friends spoke of the meaning of friendship and the need to appreciate the friends that you have. But they were still numb, still in disbelief.

"The part of the service I remember the best is when this random guy got up in front of everyone to speak," said Nicole, "and began making these weird noises. It was just the thing that Courtney would have loved. It would have cracked her up. That's all I could think of."

Courtney's death had an electrifying effect on young people, some of whom never even knew her. For weeks we heard from them.

A young man whose name we never knew came by the house to drop off a poem. Annie Dubrinsky, the musically gifted daughter of close friends, sat down at the piano and wrote a song about driving with the top down on a gorgeous October afternoon and thinking about the death of her friend. She put it on a cassette and brought it over.

E-mails circulated wildly, as young people tried to capture their thoughts while the fresh emotions washed over them. The story raced through the college grapevine.

When Jaime traveled to Europe the following summer, she found that as soon as she gave her name and school, anyone who was attending a college in the United States knew the story immediately.

One note delivered to me was signed simply "Cappuccino Man." The writer told me that Courtney had been his eleven-year-old son's counselor in day camp the previous summer. He idolized her, and at the end of summer she gave him her signed graduation photo as a present.

The boy insisted on coming to the funeral. Later that week, he took Courtney's picture and placed it inside his soccer jersey for his next game.

"I've never seen my son play like that in his life," his father wrote. "He is really not that great a soccer player, but he was all over the field that day and scored the winning goal. I didn't have to ask what had inspired him."

But only over the next few weeks did it gradually sink in with the Chit-Chats.

"I woke up on the morning of November 11, Courtney's birthday, and the first thing that came to me was that there was no Post-It note on my desk to remind me to make a birthday call," said Jen. "Maybe that's when it hit me. How unfair it was. The reality that I would never see her again.

"I had been studying, going on with school, trying to believe that nothing really had happened. And then it was her nineteenth birthday and she wouldn't be there to celebrate it. I got out of bed, screamed, and threw my shoes at the wall. That sounds stupid but I didn't know what else to do."

For Rachel, the reality hit one evening when she turned on the television in Boston and saw that a rerun of an old *Beverly Hills 90210* episode was on the air.

"That was our show, Courtney and I, all through school," she said. "Courtney had memorized whole chunks of dialogue from it. We'd get on the phone during the commercial breaks and talk about what had just happened on the show, and when it came back on we'd just hang up without even saying good-bye.

"I sat there and watched this old episode and I remembered all that. And as sad as I was feeling, I had to smile. Courtney could always make me smile."

Karen keeps two pictures on the wall of her room in Atlanta.

"One shows me and Courtney on the first real date we

both ever had," she says. "We doubled for a Sadie Hawkins Day dance and she was so happy—although I don't think she ever went out with that boy again.

"The other picture shows all six of us soaking wet on a picnic that we held for our class right before graduation. It was supposed to cap off our senior year, and the weather was horrible and everyone had to run inside with the food. But we didn't care. We were such a tight group. Whatever happened it was always us, and Courtney was the one who held it all together. But we didn't realize that until afterwards, when we'd get together again and realize that something was missing."

Bekah found herself changed in surprising ways by Courtney's death.

"I've become more like my mom," she says. "I worry over little things that I had always just assumed would turn out all right before. But I put my problems in perspective, too. I was able to tell myself that in the greater scheme of things, what did they amount to? I'd already experienced the worst that could happen.

"It's brought me and Nicole closer together, too. Because we were the ones at Michigan, we had to listen to all the stuff about how Courtney had killed herself, and how she'd been suicidal for years. We defended her all the time, and even though that was exhausting we knew it was the right thing to do. We call each other twenty times a day now."

The loss of Courtney also goaded Bekah's dad into action. Dr. Phil Parker is a practicing psychiatrist. When he heard the University of Michigan was forming a committee to look into campus drinking, he joined as the parents' representative.

"I guess I've turned into the gadfly," he said. "I keep on pumping for some sort of meaningful action. It's just too important an issue to let it slide behind a wall of academic jargon."

After the funeral, the five girls came back to our house and went into Courtney's room, where they had gathered so many times over the years. They closed the door behind them, sat in a circle, and began to express how they felt about each of the others.

"Courtney never knew how special she was to all of us," says Jen. "How much we loved her. So we had to make sure that the rest of us heard the words being said. You have to tell the people you love how much you care about them, because it can all end before you get the chance. You never know when it'll be too late. That's what her death taught us.

"I saw her when I went up to Ann Arbor the weekend before she died. She was walking to the shower in her dorm, waved good-bye, and said something like, 'I'll see you in a few weeks.'

"You don't even think twice when you're eighteen and you say something like that, do you? But now I do. Nothing is guaranteed for you. It's crucial to live for every moment. Courtney sure did."

In a few years, plans and changes will carry the Chit-Chats apart. Try as they might, the ties will weaken. This is how it happens in life.

But one of the things that will bind them together is the shared memories of the friend who couldn't share the rest of the journey with them. She will always remain in their minds as they once were, and keep a part of them forever young.

———∞———

As I mentioned earlier, six pallbearers served at Courtney's funeral. The last one came from a different compartment of her life, her summers at Camp Walden, in northern Michigan.

Jessica Steiner started at Walden the same year Courtney did. They were both eight years old, the youngest campers there, and they followed the usual scenario. The doleful letters home told their parents that camp was a big mistake. They hated the place and they were never coming back. Don't even think about it.

Then they found each other and the letters stopped.

It probably would have been cheaper if they had kept writing, because the long-distance phone bills over the years to Jessica's home in Miami were staggering.

Sherry believes that having such a close friend away from home and school gave Courtney an inner confidence, a sense that she could handle anything during the year because she always had Jessica to confide in, out of her everyday life.

The four weeks together at Walden expanded to Christmas and spring vacations spent at each other's homes. It usually was Jessica's, because who wants to be in Michigan at that time of year? One Christmas, Jessie stayed with us, though, and was crushed when she encountered a December without snow. She had never seen snow before. Now she goes to college at Colgate in upstate New York, where she sees all the snow she'll ever want.

Walden was their mystical bond. For nine summers they shared this special connection, from when they were little twerps to high school seniors who ran the place.

When Jessica left a stone on Courtney's grave, she chose a rock from Walden. They had swum across the lake at camp one day and taken it from the far shore. When they returned, they brandished the rock as proof they made the swim, and then dated it. Jessica felt it belonged with Courtney now.

"We were both stupid in the same way," she says. "That was our bond. We could tell each other things we would have been embarrassed for anyone else in the world to know.

"Like a guy she knew would come into the restaurant where she was working and she'd run to the phone, call me in Miami, and say, 'I can't breathe because he's right here.' And I'd do the same thing. Anyone else would laugh their asses off, but we understood.

"When we were twelve, we took a piece of paper and signed a pact. It said that no matter what happens, what's mine is yours. That's really how we felt. I still keep it in my room at home."

The day Courtney died, Jessica was on her way back to Miami for a school break. Her parents were waiting at the airport.

"I just looked at their faces and I knew," she says. "There was nothing else it could have been. I told them before they could get the words out, and then I went hysterical.

"I think about her forty thousand times a month. She was the coolest thing ever. So gorgeous and funny and everybody loved her. And to think that someone that great thought I was cool . . . I just don't have that anymore."

They were an odd pair physically. Courtney was tiny, and Jessie is almost six feet tall. It was like watching Mutt and Jeff walking down the street. But their personal similarities and the deep affection they had for each other was obvious.

When she arrived at our home for the funeral, Jessica hugged me and whispered, "George, I don't know what I'm going to do." She was the last to leave the cemetery. Her parents waited in the car while she spent a few moments alone and left the rock at the grave.

"I sent her a high school graduation wish," she says. "It said that my best wish for her would be for her to make just one more friendship as strong as ours. There's been so much I've wanted to tell her since then, and I have to stop myself when I reach for the phone and say, 'Whoa, can't do that anymore.'

"You know, her time was too brief, but Courtney was the happiest person I've ever known. She had the absolute perfect life.

"I don't know exactly what she'd be doing with her life right now. But whatever it was, she'd be having fun."

———✺———

A few years ago, Sherry bought our daughters matching sweatshirts that she found while on vacation. The message on the front read: "Sisters at birth, Best friends for life."

The girls flatly refused to wear them.

"They were so cheesy," says Jaime. "But it was more than that. Because there was a long time when Courtney and I weren't really friends.

"Maybe it was because the difference in our ages was a little awkward. It was about thirty months. Not close enough to be going through the same experiences at the same time, but too close for Courtney really to think of me as being older and wiser. So there were a lot of stupid fights."

Jaime was always trying to fill the role as big sister, even before Courtney came home from the hospital at four days old. Sherry meticulously had packed a suitcase with the things that the baby was going to wear home, including a very sharp bundling suit, since it was late fall.

But Jaime found the suitcase, and in her efforts to be helpful she carefully unpacked it, putting the little suit back in the right drawer. Unfortunately, I did not make this discovery until I arrived at the hospital and opened up an empty suitcase. Sherry, to put it mildly, was not pleased at wrapping her newborn in a hospital blanket for the ride home. Courtney didn't seem to mind, though.

So it went through their childhood. Courtney would often copy her big sister. She'd watch the same TV shows, read the same books, listen to the same CDs. But she'd never give Jaime the satisfaction of letting her know she was doing it.

"Once I looked in a memory book that she had started writing things in," says Jaime, "and I saw that she had copied all the stuff I had put in my own book. But Courtney never would have acknowledged that.

"It started to change the summer before she started at Michigan. I was doing an internship in Washington, D.C., and she called to tell me what classes she had registered for. I told her that she had signed up for all the wrong classes and that it was going to be a disaster.

"She got mad and I got mad, and we ended up hanging up on each other. Then I realized that I was really being a bitch, so I called her right back. We ended up talking for an hour, something we'd never done before. From that time on, I think, our relationship was different.

"When she got to Ann Arbor, she really needed me for advice. And then it ended, and we never got to be the friends we should have been.

"I like the person I am now better than at any other time in my life, and I think a lot of that has to do with Courtney's death. I see problems more clearly and put it in perspective when things go wrong. I'm less tolerant of petty people. But I'd rather have my sister.

"I'm afraid that I'm forgetting all the little things about her that made her so funny and unique. I try to write them down when they occur to me, but there are some things I just can't get down.

"I'm in a relationship that I hope will last for a long time. When we were both home, it was very important to me that we visit Courtney's grave and that I could tell him about her. He says that he thinks he knows her through me. It's important for me to be with people who knew her."

Jaime was always sure that as she and Courtney grew older they would grow closer. They would get together and talk about all the childhood memories they shared, things no one else in the world would know about, long after Sherry and I had gone. Now that won't be there for her, and I think it frightens her a little.

She spent a few moments alone with Courtney at the funeral home and slipped a written message into the coffin. She never told me what it said and I never asked. But after two years, she told me what she had written:

"Sisters at birth, Best friends for life."

CHAPTER 13

The police investigations began wrapping up around Christmas. Two public safety officers from the university came to the house and told me their findings.

No surprises there. They had concluded it was an accident. The university also promised an independent investigation to try and recreate the conditions that led to Courtney's fall. Since the university would be paying for it, however, I wondered how independent that investigation would be. It was the skeptical, cranky old newspaper guy in me.

In January, however, I received a call from the Washtenaw County Prosecutor's Office. This one contained a major jolt.

Aside from the details of the fall itself, we already had a pretty good idea of what happened on the night of Courtney's death.

She had gone to carry-in ceremonies at about 10 P.M. In this ritual, the pledges of a fraternity are carried through the front door of their house by members of a campus sorority (or sometimes vice versa). In this case, Chi Omega was the sorority, and the frat house was Phi Delta Theta.

The ceremony lasted about two hours. Then it was time to party.

Both Chi Omega and Phi Delta Theta had signed no-drinking pledges with their national chapters. Both houses were supposed to be alcohol-free. The only way the fraternity was permitted to return from a campus suspension, in fact, was by agreeing to the pledge. Moreover, the national organization had sent a monitor to Ann Arbor from its offices in Oxford, Ohio, to keep an eye on things.

But the no-alcohol pledges meant nothing. Champagne and beer were in ample and convenient supply.

Friends told us that Courtney was annoyed because a boy she liked in the fraternity was ignoring her. So she initiated some close dancing with another guy and drank champagne.

By 1 A.M., she was vomiting in the frat house bathroom, a frequent consequence of imbibing cheap champagne. An hour or so later, she left for Markley Hall in a cab with two friends. When we had discussed situations that might arise on campus, Sherry and I had always stressed to Courtney that she should never go in a car with someone who had been drinking. Walking far after a party was probably not a good idea either.

Call a cab, we told her. She was following our instructions perfectly.

When she returned to the dorm, she paid a short visit to the room of a friend and then left a note on the door of another friend. Reports about her condition vary from those who saw her in this time span.

A few of them described Courtney as being "tipsy," not focused, blurry-eyed. Others said that she was speaking coherently, although she occasionally seemed to fade out.

She walked into her room at around 3 A.M. Her entry awoke her roommate, Marni, who said that Courtney was unusually loud, even boisterous. Marni was put out at being roused, but decided that as long as she was up she might as well go to the bathroom, which was located down the hall.

When she returned the lights were out, and she assumed that Courtney was asleep in her loft. In fact, she had already fallen. But since nothing had been disturbed on the window ledge, and the ladder was still in the middle of the room, between the lofts, Marni never realized anything was wrong. She went back to sleep and didn't wake up again until campus security began banging on her door at 6 A.M.

That much was known, but it explained little. If Courtney had not been blind drunk—and from the blood-level readings in the medical examiner's report and interviews with witnesses, it didn't appear that she was— then how did she go through the window?

I wasn't prepared for what the assistant prosecutor told me next. Gamma-hydroxybutyric acid, or GHB, is also known as "liquid ecstasy," or "lemons," or "great bodily harm." It is commonly described as a date-rape drug. Traces of it had been found in her blood.

It was a minuscule amount, but the drug is known to dissolve quickly after being ingested, which is its most insidious property.

Incredibly, no police agency had seen fit to mention this previously. "We don't even know that it altered her behavior," said Ann Arbor Police Department Sgt. Michael Logghe. "This doesn't explain anything to us."

Well, I'm no Columbo, but the report had bells and whistles all over it for me.

I only knew GHB through a few sensationalized news reports about how it was dropped into the drinks of unsuspecting women. When they woke up they had no recollection of having engaged in sex. It was the perfect sleazoid crime.

Moreover, it had the tendency to enhance the effect of small amounts of alcohol and to remove inhibitions. Some women took it voluntarily to get into a party mood quicker. More commonly, because it is odorless and colorless, the drug could be given to women without their knowledge.

Close dancing with a boy she barely knew? That didn't sound like her. But it did if she had been drugged.

Behaving erratically even though she hadn't drank that much? It didn't compute. But it did if she had been drugged.

The Ann Arbor cops didn't think this was important?

When I phoned *48 Hours* correspondent Erin Moriarty with this information, two days before the segment on Courtney was to air, she made sure that it was added in a spoken postscript.

The show, in fact, fully justified my confidence in CBS. Its news crew behaved with sensitivity and high standards. I think when they first came to the story, the producers thought it was going to be another example of binge drinking. Unlike some Detroit media, however, the facts convinced them otherwise, and they made that explicitly clear.

The segment began with the words, "Courtney Cantor was a daughter that any family would be proud of." I was very grateful for that and for the slant that even the best of kids can run into unanticipated disaster connected to drinking.

The GHB finding altered that aspect of the story even further, but the show to its credit included the finding anyhow. That's called responsible journalism, and it's so rare these days that it should be on the endangered species list.

Perhaps Courtney had taken the drug herself. But as I talked to her closest friends over the next few days, they dismissed that possibility as exceedingly unlikely.

"If she had even been thinking of taking a drug like

that," said Jessica Steiner, "she would have been e-mailing and phoning everybody for weeks to get their opinions."

"Courtney was the last person I know who would rush into something like that on the spur of the moment," Bekah Parker told me. "It would have been totally out of character."

One theory holds that small amounts of GHB are made naturally by the body. But in combination with her erratic behavior during the evening, behavior she had never exhibited before, that answer didn't seem plausible.

So someone, in all likelihood, slipped it into her drink. But if anyone at the party knew how it got there, they weren't talking.

From the day after my daughter's death, the young gentlemen of Phi Delta Theta had convinced themselves that they were the victims in this affair. They refused to cooperate with any of the police investigations. Instead, they agreed among themselves to be bound by a brotherhood of silence, like a mafiosi vow of *omerta*.

In the days after Courtney's death, I had actually felt some sympathy for these young men. Certainly, I thought, no one had ever intended that this terrible thing would happen.

But that's before I knew that they had broken a no-alcohol pledge, that they had equipment for making phony identification right in the fraternity house and continued to use it so that they could buy alcohol even after her death, that one of them probably had given her the drug, and that their capacity for self-pity was bottom-less.

CHAPTER 14

———◇——

Drinking has been a part of university life for about as long as there have been universities. Romanticized and sanitized, the act of getting drunk on campus has come to be accepted as a youthful rite of passage, a part of every literary memoir of college years.

The Student Prince, for example, is a beloved operetta, an enduring image of merry student days at Heidelberg. Its best-remembered song is "Drink, Drink, Drink." In the other great German university town, Tübingen, the proprietress of the student tavern, Tante Emilia, is described by the locals as "more famous than the Reichschancellor."

Rudy Vallee rose to fame on the radio in the 1920s by crooning a drinking ditty from his alma mater, "The

Maine Stein Song." Cartoonist John Held Jr.'s drawings of smart young things in their raccoon coats and hip flasks were the symbol of college life in the same era— and this was during Prohibition.

In nineteenth-century America, college was regarded as part of a true gentleman's upbringing, insofar as it instructed him on how to hold his liquor. In more recent times, the inhabitants of *Animal House,* although assuredly no gentlemen, did drink a bit. It was one of the qualities meant to endear them to movie audiences, and so it did.

That college campuses are a rich source of liquid refreshment for the young is no great secret. The problem arises in that most freshmen enter the university around the age of eighteen, but most states, in their wisdom, have set the legal drinking age at twenty-one.

Almost inevitably, social situations develop in which the male is old enough to be served legally and the female is not. Youthful hormones and ingenuity being what they are, the couple urgently seeks a way around this situation. More often than not, they succeed.

The University of Michigan addresses the situation in a manner wholly consistent with the other "progressive" institutions in this country. They wring their hands at it. They run about in wide clucking circles and hope the public will accept this as effective action. They cover their behinds.

Until the 1960s, the universities did have a way to supervise student drinking and mitigate some of its worst excesses. The legal doctrine known as "in loco parentis" held that the university was empowered to act "in place of the parent," with the authority and the responsibility to exert control over minor students enrolled there.

This concept grew up in the 1920s, as an increasing number of women began attending college. Parents were uneasy at granting them the same degree of freedom they had given their sons and demanded that the colleges take a firmer hand with extracurricular socializing.

Through the 1950s at the University of Michigan, for example, women undergraduates were not permitted to live off campus, unless it was in a sorority house. Those conditions lent a certain degree of desperation to sorority rush. If a young woman wasn't accepted, she was condemned to living three more years in a cheerless dorm.

The university's president Harlan Hatcher, speaking in 1962, expressed the rationale for such restrictions: "We are constantly mindful that Michigan parents have sent us their most cherished possessions, and we are determined to fulfill our obligations in watching over these students. . . . College is a land halfway between home life and adult life for most students, and we must be careful not to make it all one or the other."

University administrators still use the same sort of warm and dewy rhetoric. But in Hatcher's era, they really meant it.

In the turbulent 1960s, however, in loco parentis was ground underfoot in the uncompromising demands for expanded student rights. Moreover, as the voting age and other legal definitions of adulthood were lowered to eighteen, defining college freshmen as minors requiring special care became increasingly difficult.

While the universities fretted publicly about this change, secretly they were relieved. With in loco parentis rendered invalid, many burdensome legal obligations fell aside.

The kids want to be on their own? So let 'em.

———— ❧ ————

For a few years, it appeared that another casualty of the

1960s would be the Greek system. At many of the top academic schools, pledging a fraternity or sorority became a mark of social backwardness. The really cool people were out in the streets, marching against Vietnam and having their noggins bashed by the cops.

The frat boy became the symbol of a discredited establishment, a moral slacker who could not recognize the urgency of the times. When George W. Bush ran for president in 2000, one of the most telling charges against him, in some minds, was that while Yale erupted in social protest in the 1960s, he did not join the marchers.

The fact that he did not see fit to participate rendered him suspect—a cad and shallow vessel in the view of many leading media profilers. The possibility that he may have disagreed with the causes of the marchers didn't seem to occur to them. Merely having belonged to a social fraternity in those times was enough to condemn him.

But when radical politics began simmering down in the late 1970s, the Greek system revived. One major reason was that it remained the most dependable source of liquor for the underaged on campus.

A survey conducted by the Carnegie Foundation in 1990 found that alcoholism was identified as the top campus problem by 82 percent of the sample. It outpaced the second highest problem, poor academic advising, by a full 10 percent.

"Students today come to college expecting to drink," said Henry Wechsler, director of the Harvard School of Public Health Alcohol Studies Program. "Colleges do have traditions where drinking is part of the culture, and that needs to be changed."

In a June 2000 interview with the Associated Press, Wechsler referred to alcohol abuse as the "little secret" of college life. Captain Dale Burke of the University of Wisconsin security police called it "the number-one problem on every college campus in this country, and I don't care how big or how small they are."

Virtually every study charting the phenomenon through the 1990s found that the focus of campus drinking, including binge drinking, was the Greek system. It was engrained in fraternity house culture.

College fraternities in the United States go back to the nation's roots. Phi Beta Kappa was founded at William and Mary in the landmark year of revolution, 1776, and it inspired a host of imitators immediately after the war. Fraternities were originally supposed to be academic honors and literary societies, but that began to change by the mid-nineteenth century.

Social historian J. C. Furnas places the origin of the switch at New York's Union College in the 1820s. Fraternities there became a way of formalizing one's social position and served as a base of power for campus politics. Living and dining together, the members found a way to separate themselves from the lower classes on campus, in a society that was both secret and exclusive. The idea was irresistible.

Furnas describes them as "unwitting counterparts to the men's societies of the preliterate village," not quite the scholarly ideal. Their rise had the effect of shattering the concept of the university as a unified academic community. By the time administrators grasped the consequences, however, the battle already was lost. Influential and wealthy alumni, who usually had been members of a fraternity, resisted any attempt to bar them.

Moreover, their practical benefits could not be questioned. They were the quintessential business networking tool. Friendships formed in a college fraternity house or Ivy League club endured profitably into adult life.

As colleges went coeducational, the Greek system

began to fill another function. They were marriage marts. Since the overwhelming majority of them were restrictive as to race and religion, parents could be confident that their children would be meeting and dating the "right kind" of potential mate.

One of the best-sellers of the 1940s was a book called *Take Care of My Little Girl*. It was meant to alert parents to the harmful effects of sorority snobbery and exclusion. A movie, starring Jeanne Crain, was made of the book in 1949 and enjoyed a successful run. But it didn't change anything.

By the mid-twentieth century, the system was too powerful a marketing tool for universities. They had learned to stress campus extracurriculars as their most appealing attribute.

The system became especially entrenched at Miami University in Oxford, Ohio. This remains one of the Midwest's most charming campuses, and it was a hotbed of fraternities in the nineteenth century. At one time, it was estimated that one-sixth of all the members of Greek organizations in America belonged to one that had originated at Miami.

Five still maintain their national headquarters there. Among them is Phi Delta Theta.

Founded in 1848, Phi Delta Theta is housed in an imposing structure modeled after the Governor's Palace in Williamsburg, Virginia. A member of its charter class at Miami was Benjamin Harrison, who became the twenty-third president of the United States.

Phi Delta Theta is one of the country's most respected and influential fraternities, and in 1994 the national organization enlisted all chapters in a pledge of abstention from alcohol on fraternity property.

The national group might as well have been howling into the wind, at least when it came to the University of Michigan chapter.

CHAPTER 15

I drank in college. Not a lot, unless you count the time I had a date with the young woman who had just decided to leave the convent.

I felt the situation demanded it, however, and she was very understanding about driving me home after I zonked out in the back seat of her car. I heard later that she decided to reenter the convent, and I sincerely hoped it wasn't on my account.

I never belonged to a fraternity, though. Wayne State University was an urban school where the Greek system was weak and its members regarded with a certain degree of ridicule, at least by my small circle of smart-ass friends. The student newspaper was my fraternity, and in the other reporters and editors I found kindred spirits.

I learned more than journalism there because it was such a diverse group that included veterans attending school on the GI Bill, older than most of us and far richer in experience. The newspaper was the first time I had worked with African Americans. A broad band of economic, religious, and ethnic backgrounds were represented—certainly more than could be found in any fraternity in the early 1960s.

And we all drank to some degree, either at parties or on slow afternoons when Paula took pity on us and decided not to check our IDs at the Alcove Bar, around the corner from the newspaper office.

On Friday nights, after putting the Monday paper to bed, we would walk across the street from the print shop to the Crosstown Bar. The proprietor depended on printers for his trade, so if we entered the place with them we'd always be served.

Those guys could knock down beers even faster than they could set type, and they would insist on buying new rounds for us as soon as they finished their own drinks. That pattern left most of us with three or four untouched bottles lined up in front of our chairs by the end of the evening. For years afterwards, I couldn't stand the taste of

Blatz, because that was the beer of choice at the Crosstown, and the pressure was always on to finish the bottles in front of you.

I bring up this revolting memoir of my college days only to point out that my own experience made me a realist about campus drinking. I knew it was going to happen. We thought the best way to prepare our daughters for the reality of what they would encounter was to stress moderation rather than abstinence.

That's why we had counseled Courtney to call for a cab if she had too much to drink. It was better if she did not drink at all, of course, but if she did we wanted her to be safe.

Although I didn't know it, this approach is also preferred by one of the leading researchers into campus drinking, Dr. G. Alan Marlatt, who is the director of the Addiction Behavior Research Center at the University of Washington.

He works with binge drinkers and tries to find the most effective way of dissuading them. He determined that a forty-five-minute individualized motivational session for freshmen, which emphasized responsible drinking, seemed to offer the best promise. His study was aimed especially at students planning to enter a fraternity or sorority, because his statistics showed that they were at higher risk.

"We are first trying to reduce the health risks of binge drinking by having the students understand its negative effects," he says, "such as hangovers, embarrassment, weight gain, and blackouts."

A majority of students in Marlatt's program showed a decline in drinking-related problems over the five-year duration of the study, in contrast to overall figures indicating that problem drinking is holding steady on most campuses.

In fact, the Institute for Social Research at the University of Michigan charted a small "bounce-back" in the drinking statistics starting in 1996, after about a decade of slight decline. Lloyd Johnston, the Institute's director, said the rebound occurred because efforts to address the problem seemed to have diminished, on the mistaken assumption that the problem had been solved.

Moreover, the Harvard School of Public Health found that four out of five residents of fraternity and sorority houses could be classified as binge drinkers, and that a disproportionate number of these students were under the age of twenty-one.

It would seem to be a matter of simple logic, therefore, that if universities want to address the problem of underage drinking in any meaningful fashion, they might begin by rethinking their relationship with the Greek system on their campuses.

Unfortunately, most universities cannot bring themselves to take this step, for a variety of reasons.

For one thing, universities are in competition for market share among top students. While no school that takes itself seriously wants to be known for the quality of its partying, neither does an institution want a reputation as one that cracks down hard on drinking. Nobody loves a party pooper.

Even the University of Chicago, which is about as serious as they come, advised its students in 1998 to loosen up a little, spend a bit more time away from the library. Chicago's reputation as a grind school was deadly for academic recruiting.

The students also would be infuriated at such a crackdown. After Courtney's death, word circulated repeatedly on the Michigan campus that the authorities were going to use the incident as a pretext for tougher rules on drinking. Students made it clear that any such effort would be resented and resisted.

One columnist on the *Michigan Daily* expressed senti-
ments that seemed to reflect the thinking of most students.

"The real and lasting tragedy of Courtney Cantor's
death (for us that is, not her family) is that most of the
steps taken by Authority Figures, and all of the macho,
prick-waving on the part of the Ann Arbor Police Department, won't prevent a similar accident," wrote James Mil-
lier. "When a student dies in circumstances like Cantor's
the first question is: 'What are we going to do about it?'
Answer: Nothing that will work.

"Remember how they pistol-whipped the hapless Phi
Delts for hosting the party at which Cantor received her
drinks? . . . Administrators, cops and parents. Are your
actions for our safety, or your Puritanical piece [*sic*] of
mind?"

A less belligerent *Daily* columnist, Jeff Eldridge,
thought along the same lines.

"Using the incident to make negative inferences about
the Greek system is just plain wrong," he wrote. "It
strikes me as a sort of finger-pointing intended to bring
closure to the incident, as though punishment will bring
cleansing. But disciplinary measures and blame . . . cer-

tainly won't prevent it from happening again. . . . Using Cantor's death to condemn underage drinking or punish a fraternity house demotes a puzzling and affecting tragedy to a platitude."

The message is quite clear. If students choose to break the law, you can do nothing about it. In fact, it's none of your damn business.

That is, more or less, what the father of one of the Phi Delts also told Ann Arbor police investigators. The official police report notes that this father called long distance to berate the cops for using the boys as scapegoats, and advised them to drop the line of investigation tying the fraternity to Courtney's death.

I repeat once more: The fraternity broke the law by buying liquor with phony IDs, which were made right at the house, and then by serving booze to minors. They broke their own promise to their national organization and the university. They may have had drugs on the premises.

The national organization sent a monitor to the Ann Arbor chapter to oversee their conduct and make sure they were living up to their promises. But he inexplicably decided to leave on the night of October 16, when the likelihood of alcohol being served was extremely high.

But for some strange reason everybody keeps picking on the Phi Delts. The poor, dear boys.

Another reason universities may not care to move too vigorously to enforce the laws is a matter of simple economics.

For insights into this situation I am indebted to Robert D. Honigman, an author and attorney who has documented the relationship between university housing and the capital budgets of contemporary research institutions. In personal conversation, and in his book, *University Secrets,* Honigman makes a compelling argument that the universities have a strong vested interest in keeping the Greek system functioning.

"The dorms are holding tanks for incoming freshmen, with all the qualities and warmth of a public terminal," says Honigman, "because building residence halls that are actually comfortable and reasonably priced is against the best interests of the institution.

"First of all, that would be an expensive proposition. When it comes to budget priorities, underclassmen are a nuisance. It's research facilities and the graduate schools where the grant money is, and that's where the capital investment goes."

So what you have usually is floor after floor of rectangular cells arranged along a common hallway, with the toilet at the end of the hall. At many schools, including the University of Michigan, the size of the rooms has actually been reduced since the 1930s, barely staying within minimum state standards for the health and welfare of occupants. Despite all the rhetoric about campus "community," Honigman says, the dorms are miserable places by design. (Incidentally, when the university's marketing surveys turned up the fact that it was losing many promising students because of its abominable dorms, a construction program for new living facilities was announced in mid-2000.)

The university wants the students out of the dorms by their sophomore year. It's the only way they will have enough room to house the next batch of freshmen without being forced to build more dorms.

The best way to clear the dorms is through the Greek system. If the university knows that a certain percentage of sophomores will reside in fraternity and sorority houses, existing dorms remain adequate.

As juniors and seniors, most students will then move on to private housing. That lodging probably will end up being no more expensive than the charges for a dorm room, with the added benefit of being able to prepare one's own food instead of relying on the execrable meals served to people who must remain on campus.

So it is absolutely in the university's financial interest to make sure the Greek system works. This analysis also provides insight into why so many colleges permit the abomination of freshman rush.

Some of the worst excesses of rush have been removed at the University of Michigan, at least on the books. Fraternities and sororities can no longer discriminate by race or religion, and every sorority pledge must visit each house.

Hazing is also forbidden, although this is honored more in the breach than in the observance by some fraternities.

But the social pressures of rush remain. For an entering freshman—still struggling to become acclimated to living away from home for the first time, still coping with demanding classes, still a bit nervous about all these new experiences tumbling upon her or him all at once—the pressures can be severe.

"One senses that many of these students are searching, in some cases rather desperately, for something to hold on to," writes Arthur Levine of the Carnegie Foundation in *When Dreams and Heroes Died.* "This is mirrored in the rash of books on mysticism, Marx, religion, exercise, sex, health and self-help that have become so popular among them. . . .

"Pressure and despair—the environment could not be more supportive of alcoholism if we had planned it."

In the midst of this personal turmoil, the freshman is plunged into a culture in which drinking is not only expected but encouraged. A handful of large universities, however, have tried to do more than conduct ineffectual studies. They have attempted to take action.

Among them is another Big Ten school, Indiana University. The Bloomington campus is sprawling and highly social—a place so beautiful that on a visit back after graduation, composer Hoagy Carmichael was moved to write "Stardust."

Indiana University bars rush for first-semester freshmen women, although it is permitted for men. That would seem to put the school in hazy legal territory on two fronts: interfering with the constitutional right of freedom of association and gender discrimination. But that's IU policy.

"The sororities themselves have mandated the tradition for putting off rush until second semester," says Dean of Students Richard McKaig. "They feel that it is important for a young woman to establish a grade point average and get to know her way around the campus a bit before committing to a sorority.

"We are more than happy to go along with that plan. We are less happy with the longer pledge period the fraternities impose. But if we heard opposition from the faculty we'd be prepared to open a conversation on pushing back their rush period, too.

"More and more often this is coming up now in college conferences," says McKaig. "The private schools, of course, can do pretty much what they want. But our sense is that if a case is presented by a public university for delaying rush because of academic considerations, it will withstand a legal challenge. Let's put it this way: Such a policy has not yet been challenged successfully in the courts."

Universities do have the power to suspend a Greek organization if it breaks the law or runs afoul of campus rules. So it seems reasonable that the university would also have the authority to set parameters for membership. Having the power to evict without the power to regulate would seem to make no sense. But I forget myself. We're talking about the law.

By the start of the September 2000 school year, one out of every five fraternities in the United States had declared themselves dry. Explained Jon Williamson, executive vice president of the North American Intrafraternity Conference, "I think fraternities looked at themselves and said, 'Our values are not about alcohol. So why is alcohol at the center of what we do?'"

Or perhaps the culture change resulted from skyrocketing insurance rates for these organizations because of lawsuits arising from drinking mishaps on fraternity property.

College administrators are also dubious about how much of the new campus prohibition is cosmetic, intended to mollify parents and school officials.

"I think there is a consensus among some students that this thing won't be enforced," the assistant dean for student affairs at Washington and Jefferson College told the *Pittsburgh Post-Gazette*. "And if it is enforced, then they won't get caught."

Consider, too, the role the media plays in all of this by sending decidedly mixed messages about campus drinking.

On one part of the evening news, the local station deplores the practice. Five minutes later, there is a live pickup from a campus bar where students have gathered to cheer on the team in The Big Game.

The more raucous things get, the better the news director likes it. Students are encouraged to hold up their glasses and bottles to the cameraman and shout.

The message here is quite plain. Real college sports fans drink until they puke on their shoes.

On the occasions when things grow a little out of hand and youthful drunks start tipping over cars and breaking windows and setting fires, well, then we revert back to message number one. This is deplorable! Shame on you all!

No wonder the kids smirk at adult hypocrisy.

The fact is, however, that most approaches to controlling campus drinking just don't seem to work. Universities that have invoked a zero-tolerance policy on alcohol have found an immediate upsurge in drug use. Among the drugs that have come into prominence at these places is GHB, precisely because of its ability to enhance the effect of a small amount of alcohol.

While Dr. Marlatt's moderation program has enjoyed some success, its probable application is limited. Think about what is being said to these students: Please break the law only a little bit.

When the drinking age is set at twenty-one, counselors who advise moderation become complicit in an act of legal defiance. To expect a student who is already engaging in an illegal act to do it moderately seems absurd. That's like being a little pregnant. It makes no sense.

The best solution, and I realize it sounds counterintuitive, is to lower the drinking to age eighteen, making it consistent with other major legal hallmarks of adulthood. Authorities could then institute programs that urge moderation, zero-tolerance driving policies, and other restrictions, while not winking broadly at breaking the law.

College students will drink, but I'm convinced that you can bring some degree of responsibility to their behavior. As a matter of academic policy, delay by a semester their introduction into a Greek culture that is imbued with alcohol. Treat students of age as full-fledged adults.

Perhaps political will is lacking for such a change. The grandstands, after all, would rather hear legislators attack any such suggestion and call for abstinence as the only real solution. But that approach just isn't realistic.

Not all Greek organizations behave irresponsibly. Some live up to what they claim to represent. Unfortunately, the Phi Delts of Michigan were not among them, nor were the women of Chi Omega who were supposed to be watching out for their young pledges.

Still, I can't help but feel that Courtney would have had a better chance of being prepared for what she encountered at the fraternity house that night if the university had done a better job of enforcing its own rules, and if the mystique—the thrill of surreptitiousness that surrounds campus drinking—had been removed.

CHAPTER 16

The nature of minyan groups is to change constantly. Ours was no different.

Some dropped out as their mourning period ended. Others attended for a month or so, feeling that was sufficient, and we never saw them again. Sam moved to Florida to be with his son.

But a few stayed on. Maybe they showed up just once or twice a week. But they were reluctant to sever this connection entirely, even though the religious obligation that brought them there had been fulfilled.

Sherry and I were among this group. We had touched something worth holding on to in the temple library. But it took me a while before I figured out what it was.

Sunday's minyan usually brought in a full house. Every space at the table was taken, and we had to set up two rows of folding chairs to boost the seating capacity.

In addition to the usual bagels and coffee, there was also smoked salmon, sliced tomatoes, and orange juice. Sometimes there was cake. Who could pass up a feast like that?

Because of the mob Sundays attracted, the leader of the service usually asked us to go around the table and identify ourselves, and maybe talk a little about something nice that had happened during the last week.

This procedure was a little too touchy-feely for the regulars. Ted would introduce himself as Franz Kafka one week, Itzhak Perlman the next. Ben would volunteer that he'd had a really terrific banana in his cereal that morning.

We felt that we really didn't need such overt displays to know how much we had come to care about each other. We understood our special bond.

We also shared another unspoken belief. We felt that for a time we had been inoculated against tragedy, that while we honored our dead we would be spared more pain. After the last Kaddish had been recited, all bets were off. Then we'd be candidates for new disasters. That was the shape of the deal we had cut with the Almighty.

We presupposed, of course, a belief in some rational design, a larger plan that we could not discern, an order within the seeming chaos of existence. The intimation of such an order is what sustained all of us.

"If losing a child does not affirm your faith in God," Dave Techner told me, "I don't know what will."

That puzzled me when he said it. In the face of terrible personal tragedy, many individuals have their faith shattered: Holocaust survivors who lost everyone they loved, brilliant young men and women afflicted with a crippling disease, upright citizens gunned down by a hopped-up thug.

How can God allow this to happen? The complaint is as old as Job.

I cannot believe in a God who goes around pushing little girls out of sixth-floor windows as part of some vast, eternal, predetermined plan. But I can wrestle with the idea of a God who was just as saddened as I was by Courtney's death. Albert Einstein said, "God is subtle, but not malicious." I believe that.

But while I was comfortable with the outer flourishes

of religious observance—the rituals and the holidays—the core of belief always had eluded me.

When Rabbi Loss led Sherry and me in prayer over Courtney's body at the University of Michigan Hospital, the words we spoke were those of the Shema, Judaism's central declaration of faith: "Hear, O Israel, the Lord is God, the Lord is One."

I had said the words hundreds of times. They were familiar to me since the earliest memories of childhood. But I could never erase my doubts about their truth. The leap that acceptance demanded was too long for me to make. They were just words.

I am, after all, a journalist—a skeptic by training and inclination. You are taught that you can only report on verifiable fact—what you see, what you touch. Rumors of distant miracles don't cut it in my business.

Any decent investigative reporter requires more documentation, more sources before handing in his copy. But I desperately wanted affirmation.

The search for more evidence sent my mind on a restless quest through old, dusty files. Oddly enough, a half-forgotten story I had written years before Courtney's death helped lead me where I wanted to go.

The article was about complexity theory. I had interviewed a leading expert in this rapidly evolving field, biophysicist Stuart Kauffman of the Santa Fe Institute. In his book *At Home in the Universe,* Kauffman argued that his work had convinced him it was mathematically impossible for life on Earth to have arisen by blind chance.

He said there are two thousand enzymes that support life, and the chance of assembling them randomly is about one in 10 to the 40,000th power. "The likelihood of that happening," he said, "is like a tornado sweeping through a junkyard and assembling a Boeing 747 from the materials there."

The other possible explanation is the existence of a spontaneous internal order, a self-organizing mechanism that sustains life and is common to every complex system in the universe.

"I look out my window," said Kauffman, "and according to the science I read, I expect to see a world filled with disorder. A steady loss of energy, a winding down, entropy. Yet wherever I look there is order. That is what needs explaining. That is the science that needs to be invented."

Kauffman stopped short of claiming a proof of God

through computer models and mathematical formulae. Yet there was a cartoon near his office showing a young man pouring something into a beaker, with feathers flying all over the place and some kind of indescribable glop on the table.

The caption read: "God as a kid on His first try at creating chickens."

So if people choose to infer the existence of a Creator from his work, that this existence is the ultimate meaning of the order he found within complexity, Kauffman would not object.

At the time, this article was just another assignment to knock off for the Sunday paper. But now I found a deeper resonance in it.

I went back and reread the book and found Kauffman's reasoning both convincing and reassuring, yet I needed something more. Not only a second source, but maybe some evidence of a miracle or two, just to clinch the case. Any little miracle would do.

That's when I came across a short poem about miracles written by Rabbi Abraham Ibn Ezra, a Spanish-born scholar and writer of the twelfth century. The verse seemed to be addressed directly to me.

He wrote about how we insist upon looking for miracles to confirm our belief in God. Yet we ignore what we see before us daily.

In wonder-workings or some bush aflame
We look for God and fancy You concealed.
But in earth's common things you stand revealed
While grass and flowers and stars spell out Your name.

There is a big gap in time and certainly in context between Kauffman and Rabbi Ibn Ezra. But I think they are saying the same thing.

God is within us and among us. Look around. All the proof we need is in everything we see, every breath we take.

These were my sources. Maybe the path to belief wasn't opened to me quite as neatly as it sounds in the telling. But the quiet rationality of these two men was a landmark for me, beacons of understanding.

If I hadn't come to believe that somehow, in a way I cannot comprehend, we will be together again, the pain of losing my daughter would have been unbearable. In the face of such terrible things, faith is all that you have.

The alternative is a bitter hopelessness that drains our days of meaning.

I don't know if I would have reached this foothold had it not been for Courtney's death. In searching restlessly for consolation, in my need to find some meaning, in the minyan prayers in the temple library, I had at last found and embraced the core of my faith.

———— ∽ ————

We were stunned to learn, however, that God doesn't always hold up His end of the bargain.

About halfway through our time as minyan regulars, Kenny came into the library one morning, his face pale, a distracted look in his eyes. After services, he took me aside.

"I found out yesterday that I need bypass surgery," he said. "And they want me to have it right away. You want to know the truth? I'm scared shitless."

Any normal person would be. Kenny was not yet fifty, still trying to pull out of the depressed state of mind into which the death of his father had flung him. They were in business together, having established a lucrative niche in the insurance market by selling malpractice protection to lawyers.

"When I lost my dad I lost my business partner and my best friend, along with my father," he said. "It took me months before I could look forward to going into the office.

"We had season tickets for the Detroit Lions as long as I can remember, and we always went to the games together. I wanted to give them up. I had no taste for it anymore. My kids made me go to the Thanksgiving Day game because that was always the biggest one of the season for Grandpa. But it was tough to walk into that stadium without him.

"He died in my arms. I never thought I'd be looking at my own mortality so soon."

A few days later, he came to services with a gift, a gold neck chain in the shape of the Hebrew word *Chai*. It means "Life." The chain had been given to someone years before as he went in for major surgery. When he came through it, he gave the chain to a friend facing a similar operation.

Since then the gift had been passed on from friend to friend, both Jewish and Christian. And the story was that everyone who wore the *Chai* came through their surgery all right.

The thought seemed to comfort Kenny. So did the prayers recited on his behalf by our minyan group. There is a place in the daily service when we say a *Mi She-beirach,* or a prayer for healing. In many congregations, the names of the persons for whom the prayer is intended are said silently. At Temple Israel, the custom is to name them out loud.

Some of the lists ran to a dozen names or more, because it is intended not only for the physically infirm but for those struggling with spiritual ailments, too. So every morning we spoke Kenny's name in our prayers.

"You have no idea what it feels like to be sitting at that table and hear the prayers coming around it, all of them being said for you," he told me. "I've never felt that sort of strength inside me before."

Still, as the day of the operation approached, he grew increasingly apprehensive. Sherry and I had dinner with Kenny and his wife, Nancy, a week before the surgery. When the bill came I, quite uncharacteristically, picked it up.

"I'm getting this one," I told him. "And right after you get out of the hospital, I expect to be reciprocated."

He laughed, thanked me for my vote of confidence, and said it was a promise. But it didn't help at all when, on the scheduled morning of the operation, he instead showed up at minyan. He explained that it had to be delayed by a day because of some mix-up at the hospital. The change hardly soothed his nerves.

By his unexpected appearance, Kenny almost spoiled his surprise. He had told us that after the surgery, he had to turn over the *Chai* to someone else. He wasn't allowed to keep it. That was the deal.

That didn't seem fair to Sherry. So on the morning of his expected operation she was in the middle of collecting money from everyone in the group to buy Kenny a permanent *Chai*. We barely managed to cover up what was afoot.

When the phone call from Nancy came a few days later, telling us that everything had turned out fine, Sherry went out and bought the chain. We all agreed that there was no sense tempting any dark angels by buying it before we received that call.

A few weeks later, when he was feeling strong enough, Kenny came back to minyan and was presented with his very own *Chai*.

He cried. We all cried.

But we would soon learn that Kenny was not the only one of our group who would be shaken out of his mourning by death's discreet tap on the shoulder.

CHAPTER 17

———∾———

One year and three weeks after Courtney's death, the University of Michigan informed me that it had wrapped up its engineering study of the accident. I was invited to Ann Arbor to see the results.

In a meeting room near the university legal counsel's office, I was shown a slide presentation that a Massachusetts-based consultant had put together. He had recreated several possible placements of her body in relation to the loft and the window, and had experimented with various positions that could have led to the fall.

His conclusion? The only possible way that her center of gravity could have shifted far enough forward to propel her through the open window was if she had been kneeling on the inside ledge.

This theory had just one problem, the same one I had with the wacko conspiracy theorist. If she had fallen from the ledge, the items resting upon it—a window fan and a CD player among other things—would presumably have been knocked askew.

But from all the photographic and written documentation that we had obtained, no evidence existed of any disturbance. Nothing on the ledge, not even the dust, was touched. Moreover, there was no trace of vomit outside the window or on the ground below, and the only conceivable reason for her to be kneeling on the ledge with her head out the window was if she was being sick.

So this demonstration really explained nothing, but I understood why the university had enthusiastically embraced this theory. Three months before, I had filed a lawsuit for negligence in the construction of the window.

The decision to sue was the most difficult decision I'd made in the months after my daughter's death. For a variety of reasons, I took no satisfaction in suing the University of Michigan.

Winning lawsuits against public universities is extremely difficult. In most instances, they are protected by sovereign immunity. This principle, embedded deeply in the common law, holds that no government body may be sued, unless it gives consent, for anything that may occur as a result of carrying out its official functions.

But among the exceptions are personal injury resulting from negligence and breach of contract.

Because I feared that the university's investigation would end up precisely where it did—in a small puddle of goo—I went ahead and hired an attorney.

Another reason I was reluctant to pursue legal action is that the University of Michigan has an incredibly strong hold on its alumni, and Michigan has more alumni than any other American college.

A haze of nostalgia surrounds their memories of bright college days. They treasure their years in Ann Arbor, which has been described as the quintessential college town. That description is pretty close to being accurate.

Football Saturdays in Ann Arbor are a celebration unlike any other, and the Wolverines, who haven't suffered a losing season since 1967, inspire a devotion that goes beyond simple zeal. Otherwise normal people live and die over the performances of a bunch of teenagers. Even people with no particular tie to the university feel an allegiance because of their loyalty to the football team. Tears come to their eyes when they watch the marching band come stepping out of the north end zone roaring "The Victors" in a pregame ritual that no one would ever dare to change.

When a conservative public interest group gathered data indicating that the university's race-conscious admission policies could be in violation of the Constitution, and that the university had lied about implementing these policies, no in-state attorney would take the case. You don't tangle with the Wolverines in Michigan.

The attorney I retained, Darrel Peters, was a rare combination, having received degrees in both engineering and law. If the window in Courtney's room was inherently unsafe, he was in the unique position of being able to understand why and of doing something about it.

Another attorney had told me that no one was an expert in defenestration. That wasn't the sort of personal injury case one often encountered. Darrel's specific area of expertise, in fact, was automotive, and he had won several major judgments from the Big Three automakers.

But I needed to know the mechanics and construction of that window, and I felt that he was the best lawyer to figure it out. Once I witnessed the university's self-serving demonstration, I was doubly glad I'd made the move. If we simply accepted the premise that she had indeed fallen through the window while kneeling forward on the ledge, the university would have been in the clear. The accident would have been a direct result of Courtney's own negligence.

What I had not been prepared for, however, was the intensity of the personal criticism that followed news of the lawsuit. Suddenly everyone was an expert in this case.

People who had no idea about the facts beyond what they had read and heard in the initial media reports knew absolutely that there was no negligence here. Courtney had fallen to her death because she was blind drunk. Moreover, because she had been drinking while under the legal age, she basically got what was coming to her. We are all responsible for the consequences of our own actions, and being dead would teach her a good lesson.

Another well-wisher told me that my lawsuit was contemptible and, moreover, I was being punished by God for having "gloated" about the gun deaths of black children in the city. Needless to say, no such article even remotely resembling that was ever written.

After twenty years as a columnist, you become used to strongly stated disagreements with your opinions. If you don't hear them, you're not doing your job.

Most of the time I laugh them off. Some I answer. The few that come in unsigned I immediately toss in the wastebasket. I have no time for people who don't have the guts to give their names but want to call me every name in the book.

But I was stunned by the venom that came in now. It seemed that everyone who ever was angered by one of my columns in the past saw the chance to nail me with a cheap shot by invoking my daughter's death.

My favorite came from a guy who disagreed with a column I wrote about how the excesses of the 1960s still color our attitudes toward sex, divorce, and parental responsibility. He wrote that the death of my child had obviously driven me crazy and that my "frivolous" lawsuit offered proof.

I answered none of these letters. But each time an especially malicious one came in, I made a charitable contribution to Courtney's scholarship fund in the name of the letter-writer and made sure he was sent a notification. I knew that if Courtney had been there to read the letters, she would have been convulsed with laughter.

But the nasty response was worth the price. Because as Darrel concluded his own investigation, we felt that we were finally seeing a clearer picture of what had happened on the night of October 16.

Courtney was not intoxicated. We were sure of that. Her drinking had not reached anywhere close to that level of impairment.

But we had reason to believe that she had been given GHB, which would have accounted for her erratic behavior during the fraternity party. The effects of the drug had not worn off by the time she returned to Markley Hall.

She was very tired when she climbed into her loft at 3 A.M. and still a little fuzzy-headed from GHB's effects. After Marni left the room, Courtney was chilled. The day had been warm and the window was open, but as often happens in mid-October the temperature plummeted after the sun went down. It was in the mid-forties that night.

Since GHB accentuates the feelings of heat and cold, she probably felt uncomfortable enough to want to shut the window. The ladder, however, had been left in the middle of the room, making it tough to climb down.

In her hazy state of mind, Courtney apparently decided it would be a good idea to crawl out on the cross-beam that ran from one loft to the other. Hanging by her feet, she then attempted to lean down and shut the window.

This course of action was not one that anyone with a clear head would have followed. Because of the drug, however, Courtney did not have a clear head. While she was hanging in this way, she lost her balance and plunged right through the opening in the window.

It was a one-in-a-million shot, her body lined up perfectly with the gap below her. If she had tried to do it intentionally, she probably would have hit the ledge or the sash or some other impediment and broken the fall.

That scenario also accounts for bruises found on her toes. That's where she was hanging on when she fell.

It sounds implausible. But as Sherlock Holmes pointed out, when all other explanations do not account for all the facts, the one that remains, however unlikely, must be the answer. And only this one fit.

Not that it was any consolation. It was, in fact, such an outrageously stupid accident that it only deepened our sense of despair.

But at least it was an answer, and after months and months of wondering that answer was something.

Accidents, however, are not unavoidable, and that was

the basis of our lawsuit. The action had to be filed by August 1999, because the windows would be seven years old then. Under Michigan law, no suits alleging negligence in building design could stand after that much time had elapsed.

We contended that the windows were poorly designed and situated in a way that made a fall through them a foreseeable event. The university, of course, insisted that they met all safety standards and were perfectly acceptable—although the self-admitted failure rate of one in six rendered that position somewhat questionable.

Seeing how a jury felt about it would have been interesting, but we never had the chance to find out.

The university's lawyers came upon a state Supreme Court decision, *Griffin v. City of Detroit*. The plaintiff was the estate of a woman who was a tenant in public housing. While in her bathtub, she had fallen and broken her neck.

The court ruled, however, that an apartment unit in public housing is a private dwelling. So the city was shielded from legal exposure under sovereign immunity because any harm resulting from negligence occurred in a private place.

Incredibly, in a series of advisory opinions, the Supreme Court extended this immunity to college dormitories. There would seem to be a substantial difference in privacy rights between the residents of public housing and those of a college dorm, but the court ruled otherwise. So when the University of Michigan moved for summary judgment, the judge had no recourse but to agree.

What this means, incredibly, is that a public university has no legal accountability to provide safe housing. As soon as a student moves into the dorm, all bets are off. Look out, kids. You're on your own.

I wonder how many parents understand that. If they don't, they'd better. Take nothing in those dorms for granted. If anything bad happens there and the university is called to account, its stated legal response is to scurry as fast as it can behind its shield of immunity.

When I read this decision, I immediately flashed to the great line from the Paul Newman film *The Verdict*. "If you want justice go to a whorehouse, because if you go into court you're going to get screwed."

I have no intention of detailing the pursuit of our legal battle through the darker regions of the judicial fever swamps. Dickens already has told that sort of story much better than I could. We did, eventually, pursue the suit against the university through other avenues and reached a settlement.

When someone uses the phrase "It isn't about the money," my experience is that it invariably is about the money. But the prospect of raking in a cash windfall because of the death of my daughter makes me sick. It is dirty money that I neither earned nor wanted. Whatever comes in will almost certainly go to settle Jaime's education bills.

There are times, however, when you feel that a situation is so harmful, so wrong, that you are compelled to use the legal system in an attempt to change it. If that's someone's idea of a frivolous lawsuit, so be it. To me this action was all about an effort to force universities and fraternities to face up to the consequences of their policies and actions, and choose another course.

Does Courtney share a portion of the blame for what happened? Of course she does. She shouldn't have been drinking. But measured in the overall scale of culpability, her portion is far less than that of a Greek system running out of control and a university that won't live up to the cheery promises it makes about the well-being of its students.

Because of my venture into the legal rain forest, I certainly have not come to hate the University of Michigan. But if I had it to do over again, would I choose to send my children there?

I just don't know.

CHAPTER 18

———— ❧ ————

Midge Decter, the neoconservative commentator, once wrote that the greatest moment of parenthood is "when you learn to your astonishment that there is a life more important to you than your own."

If I'd been offered that exchange, my life for my daughter's, there is no question how I would have chosen. But they didn't give me the option.

I knew that the best and most important thing I had ever been in my life was a father. And the life that was left to me had been abruptly diminished.

I became careless about a number of things. My eating habits deteriorated, and I put on about fifteen pounds in the months following Courtney's death. I quit exercising. My writing, which had been the engine that moved my life, became meaningless. I could feel the quality decline, but I didn't much care about that.

I kept telling myself that I had a lot to live for: a loving wife, a wonderful daughter, a satisfying career. None of it mattered. These are the classic symptoms of clinical depression, and I knew it. But I didn't much care about that, either.

One of the other things I let slip was my annual medical checkup.

For the previous year, I had been undergoing treatment for a rare blood disorder called Gaucher's Disease. I'd been born with it, but it hadn't turned nasty on me until I was well into my fifties.

Even then, all it did was enlarge my spleen to something like twenty times its normal size. When my doctor saw it, he grew agitated. Although he didn't tell me at the time, he suspected leukemia. But I exhibited none of the other symptoms of that disease. My problem seemed to confound the world of medicine for several weeks.

On a hunch, the oncologist to whom I was referred took a bone marrow sample, and there it was. Unmistakable Gaucher's. Treating it involved having an IV plugged into the back of my hand twice a month so that the enzyme my blood lacked could be supplied. My spleen would then behave itself, and the disease would not go on to attack my liver. This treatment would last for the rest of my life.

In my mind, I had dodged a bullet. This was inconvenient, but it sure wasn't leukemia.

Maybe that close call was on my mind when I decided to pass on my annual physical. Maybe I just couldn't handle it so close to my daughter's death. Or maybe I just remembered the minyan bargain. Nothing bad would happen to me for a while. Even Kenny's bypass surgery didn't shake my faith in that.

So more than two years passed before I went to the doctor again. Once more, he found much to be alarmed about. This time it was the reading on my prostatic specific antigen (PSA) test, the early warning sign of prostate cancer. The number was far higher than it should have been. It was, in fact, dangerously high.

He sent me in for a biopsy, but I think I knew in advance what the result would be. When it was confirmed, I could only muster a detached nod of acquiescence.

"Unfortunately, you have an especially aggressive form

of this cancer," said the urologist, "and we will treat it aggressively."

He sent me immediately to the hospital for tests: an MRI and a bone scan, to determine whether the cancer had metastasized. If it had, little could be done.

I didn't tell Sherry exactly what had been said about the seriousness of this cancer, but I think she knew.

At this point, it all seemed up for grabs. If they told me I had months to live, that I would not see the next summer, or Jaime's graduation from law school, or my grandchildren, I wouldn't have been too surprised.

I was, in fact, relaxed. Usually an MRI drives me nuts. I need a sedative when they stick me into that container and the machine descends to within inches of my head. My latent claustrophobia comes leaping out of the closet and goes screaming around the room.

But this time, I just lay on the table thinking. Composed. My concerns were for my wife and daughter and my parents. Coming so quickly after one terrible loss, I didn't want them to go through another.

What puzzled me was that I felt great mentally. For the first time in months, my perspective had shifted.

If the worst, the very worst thing, happened, I'd be

with Courtney again. I was sure of this, as sure as I knew who had won the 1968 World Series.

And if I survived? Well, then everything from now on was a bonus. Every sunset, every snowfall, every walk by the ocean, every kiss, every Thanksgiving turkey. All of them would be rediscovered treasures.

I knew all of this with calm and utter clarity as the machine took the measure of my body and processed the information that would indicate life or death.

My Aunt Shirley used to say, "There's only one thing to be afraid of, and there's no use being afraid of that because it's going to happen anyhow."

That's all very nice when you're sitting around the Sunday dinner table making conversation, feeling fit and able, ready to give the reaper the race of his life. It's something else again when you're on the hospital table waiting for the news.

Certainly I wanted to live. I knew that now, and it came as a bit of a relief. But I was no longer afraid to die.

That was Courtney's gift to me. At that point I decided that this book would be my gift to her.

———ᐒ———

The minyan group responded to the news with a hearty round of *Mi Shebeirachs* for me. Kenny had been right. When those prayers come rolling around the table with your name on them, there is an unmistakable sense of strength and comfort.

Many of the men in the group had experienced their own tussle with prostate cancer. Some of them had it surgically removed. Others had been given radioactive implants that attacked the cancer cells from within.

In fact, wherever I turned for the next few weeks it seemed that I met someone else who had gone through it. When New York's Mayor Rudy Giuliani was diagnosed with it at about the same time, I started to suspect it was in the water.

I became aware of a major debate going on about PSA testing and when the numbers should be cause for immediate treatment. Something like three out of four men will experience some form of prostate cancer, most in their later years.

Before development of the PSA test, many men went to their graves never even knowing they had prostate cancer. But many of them went to their graves because it was detected too late. Better to err on the safe side.

My medical reports came back with a gold star. The

cancer hadn't spread, although it was outside the prostate capsule. The treatment decided upon was radiation.

That sounded good to me. Radiation was the least intrusive method, and the medical center was a ten-minute drive from my office in Detroit. Moreover, one of the top men nationally in the field of radiation oncology would be directing my treatment.

Jeff Forman is the kind of physician you hope you'll have when the game is on the line. His mixture of assurance and compassion is what the best medical schools hope to implant in their graduates.

He immediately took Sherry aside and calmed her worst fears, for which I was especially grateful. Then he told me exactly what I had to look forward to.

For two weeks, I would be placed in a cyclotron. Every day for forty-five minutes I would be bombarded with neutrons to stun the cancer cells into submission. Then for the next four weeks, I would come in for ten-minute treatments, and photons would finish up the job of destroying the malignancy.

There would be thirty treatments in all, and about midway through I could expect to feel extremely fatigued. Although you're not aware of it lying passively on the table, the radiation saps a good deal of your energy.

Radiation would be combined with injections of the hormone drug Luprin to shrink the prostate and a daily dose of Casodex to clean up any lingering cancer cells.

This therapy had been pioneered by Dr. Forman, and the Detroit Medical Center was one of only two facilities in the country that had the right equipment. The other was in Seattle, which would have been a tough commute.

"I knew there had to be some good reason I decided to stay in Detroit," I told him. "I just never dreamed that this would be it."

"You mean you don't believe the Red Wings are reason enough?" said Dr. Forman. It cheered me to realize that we were on the same page in assessing the important things in life.

This conversation took place in January 2000. Before I left his office, the receptionist handed me a parking pass. Its expiration date was December 2003. That made me feel a lot better, too.

The treatment ran its course, uneventfully and—thankfully—undramatically, except for the bladder episode.

The technicians emphasized that I was to show up for each treatment with a full bladder, so that it would be situated away from the target area of the radiation. Otherwise, pal, you're looking at long-term diapers in your wardrobe.

They didn't have to tell me twice. For sixty minutes before each treatment, I guzzled bottled water for all I was worth. I would walk down the steps into the treatment area accompanied by soft splashing sounds.

But I was a bit overambitious in gauging my water capacity. It became tougher and tougher to get through the entire forty-five minutes on the cyclotron while holding everything in.

One day there was a half-hour delay before treatment started, and I knew I was in big trouble. It might have been the moaning that escaped my mouth each time the technician changed the position on the table that gave it away.

"Mr. Cantor, are you in pain?" he asked.

"No," I said, "only in distress. May I be excused?"

The treatment had to be interrupted while I relieved myself. When I scrambled back aboard the table, immeasurably refreshed, the cyclotron had to be recalibrated, a tedious procedure.

"I don't think you really need quite that full a bladder," said the technician.

I thanked him. I am by nature, however, a cautious

man. I continued to swig the bottled water, but when I heard the telltale squishing sound when I walked, I learned to cut it short.

The treatment ended on a glorious spring day in early May. I walked back to my car in the hospital lot, drove home, and immediately joined a classical CD club. I wanted to hear music that I didn't know. I wanted to make travel plans. I wanted to go to a ballgame and eat a steak and write and make love.

My life had been restored to me. Maybe it would turn out to be merely an extension on the loan. This sort of thing carries no guarantee. Every time I go in for a new PSA reading, I know that I'll be holding my breath a little.

But what a gift life is in spring. I almost had to lose mine to learn that again.

CHAPTER 19

On her grave marker we carved the words, "A Beautiful Life."

That is the literal translation of Courtney's name in Hebrew. It is also a true summation.

If we have learned one thing through this whole terrible experience—the death of a daughter and the specter of cancer—it is that all you have to hold on to are the beautiful memories of your life and your faith. Trying to get through without them is like going on a road trip without a map or a motor.

I'm not talking about memory in terms of wallowing in pools of regret. We all do too much of that.

But only when we look in the rearview mirror do we

truly understand. The problems that marred our sense of contentment when their shadows fell so large across our path will shrink. The worst terrors in life are self-inflicted, and the saddest phrase in the language is, "I was happy and didn't know it."

The chance to seize time as it passes can never be regained. Understanding that is the beginning of living wisely. Unfortunately, we often must endure a terrible loss before we learn.

Courtney's time passed much too quickly. It wasn't grasped tightly enough, and now we have only its memory. But that isn't nearly all. She left us with too many gifts to measure.

Our lives will never be what they were, but many of the changes have enriched our lives rather than destroyed them.

There is a Nat King Cole song that begins with the line: "If I had to choose just one day to last my whole life through."

I think about that now. For me it would be an August morning in 1988. We were staying in Colorado and went for a horseback ride before breakfast. It was a shining summer day in the Rockies, and the resort had set up the meal on picnic tables near a mountain creek. One of the wranglers took our picture as we sat down to eat.

Maybe it is the fact that someone took a picture of it that imprinted the moment so vividly in my mind. But there we are, the girls still wearing their riding helmets, laughing in the sunshine. Jaime was eleven, Courtney was almost nine. I can still feel the sun on my face, hear the wind up in the treetops. Our lives were as promising as the bright new day.

I keep the picture on my work desk at home. Whenever I look at it I smile. If heaven means living the happiest moment of your life eternally, I'd settle for this one.

There is also our candleholder of life. Jewish custom is to light a memorial candle on the eve of the anniversary of a death. But this holder, a gift from a friend, is meant instead to be illuminated on a birthday, because it is a celebration of life.

The copper exterior is shaped as dancing figures. So when we light the candle each November 11 and place it inside, the shadows leap and soar against the wall. It's as if it was the Snort's spirit dancing there, the way she did so often in life, and my heart dances with the flame.

There was more dancing as a gift from Marni, her

roommate. Dance was Marni's major at Michigan, and at the end of her freshman year she dedicated the number she choreographed at the class recital to Courtney. I couldn't think of a more heartfelt tribute.

Marni's father, Marshall Golden, had only known Courtney for a few weeks, but he was crushed by the accident. Just a few weeks before, he and I had been laughing and lugging furniture up to the girls' room, and now their brief friendship was over. When he and his wife came to the house before the funeral, all he could do was hug me and sob.

When he found out about the scholarship fund we had set up in Courtney's memory, Marshall went back to his computer in Minnesota, contacted everyone he knew, and asked for contributions.

By the following spring, he gave us a check for nearly ten thousand dollars. The fund was established permanently shortly afterwards, with people donating to it at a rate that astonished us. In the issue of the temple magazine that followed her death, the list of contributors ran to three pages of agate type.

The reward is the letters we receive from the recipients of the scholarship. We have no voice in making the decision on who receives the grants, which is as it should be. But each of them, some of whom Courtney had known, wrote us to express their gratitude.

Whenever one of these letters comes in, it is as if some part of Courtney remains alive.

Sherry and I make it a point to talk about her as often as we can. People seemed uncomfortable at first about bringing up the subject, but we always rushed to assure them that we wanted to talk about our daughter. We would not allow her memory to be pushed off to a corner. She will remain a central part of our lives as long as we draw breath.

In one of the last games played at Tiger Stadium, the Detroit ballclub gave me the honor of throwing out the first pitch. I was deeply touched by the gesture, not only for my sake but because it gave my dad and brother, who had watched hundreds of ballgames there, a chance to walk upon its holy ground.

But the best part of the day was that I took Courtney's mitt to the mound with me. She had worn the glove while playing on the Andover junior varsity team, and I knew that she was with me somehow as I said good-bye to the ballpark I loved so much.

My pitch wasn't a strike. It came in high and wide. I was just relieved it made it there and that my daughter was part of the day.

An old friend of mine phrased it best. We hadn't seen each other in several years, and she wanted to tell me how sorry she was about the accident. I caught her up on other parts of our lives and how Jaime had won admission to Harvard Law School.

"We really have a daughter to be proud of," I told her. She corrected me. "You have two daughters to be proud of."

And she was absolutely right. Nothing will ever change that.

The Chit-Chats and Jessica remain part of our extended family. They come to the house whenever they are back in town, and all of them make it a point to call Sherry on Mother's Day and Courtney's birthday. They are wonderful young women and fill us with pride at how well our daughter chose her friends.

We finally decided to dispose of Courtney's bed. We thought it best to take it out of her room, although Sherry made sure it was done when we were out of town.

We then moved the computer table into that space.

So I am writing this book where Courtney used to sleep. I feel good about that, and her presence still suffuses this part of the house.

The furniture has, however, confused the living daylights out of Snickers. The absence of his longtime shelter puzzled our sheltie mix for weeks. But he has discovered another serviceable spot beneath Sherry's dressing table in our bedroom. When we're out of the house during the day, or during an especially nerve-wracking thunderstorm, he retreats under there and is happy.

Now that I have gone through the spin-dry cycle of the journalistic process, my own writing has changed. I never thought of myself as a cheap-shot artist, but I sometimes went for an easy laugh at the expense of a figure in the news, just to show what a witty fellow I can be. I don't do that anymore. I've been on the receiving end of such careless jabs.

Just as I was determined not to play the part of victim, I have also tried to put aside any bitterness toward individual members of the fraternity. I would hope that in later years, as their understanding deepens, they will come to see how harmful their actions were and feel some sense of remorse.

As for the one who slipped her the GHB, let it lie on his conscience forever. That's not my score to settle.

I also have learned to tell my love. In many ways, our marriage is stronger than it ever has been. This tragedy drew us closer. Sherry and I are now each other's best friend, an element that wasn't always present in our marriage before. It surely is now.

Other relationships have improved, too. We stopped for lunch at Niagara Falls on a recent trip and I called my father at home. I wanted to tell him that we were seated in the restaurant overlooking the falls, where we had eaten so many times on car trips when I was a child.

"You won't believe it, Dad," I said, "but after all these years, the water is still falling."

I was really saying, "I love you, Dad," without using the words—much as Courtney had done with me by giving me that ferocious hug the evening I said good-bye to her at Markley Hall. I understood that then, and I knew my father did now.

Religion plays a far more important part than before, and we find ourselves drawn to people who share those values. Judaism tells us that it is our duty to repair the world. First, though, we must heal ourselves, and the way to do that is through faith. We understand that now, and our lives are better for it.

All these changes are Courtney's legacy.

———⋗———

The afternoon before her death, she left a message on my office voice mail. It came in at about 3:30, but by the time I picked it up and called back, two hours later, she had already left for dinner.

The message was simple. "Hi, Dad. I need to talk to you. Give me a call."

That was it. I never had the chance to find out what she wanted. It was probably just some help with her homework or to make a case for a few extra bucks. I'll never know. But every event that occurs is the cumulative consequence of millions of previous events. Alter the slightest part of the equation, and the outcome may be entirely different.

So I have wondered many times if I could have said anything to my daughter had I returned the call in time. Maybe not. There was nothing that I could possibly have foreseen or warned her about. No premonition or fore- shadowing.

A word of caution about the party that night. A fatherly advisory to take it slow. But a no-drinking pledge was in effect, and I had barely even heard of GHB. My parting words probably would have been, "Have a good time and get to bed at a reasonable hour." And Courtney would have laughed at my concern.

There is a passage in *The Once and Future King* in which the aged Merlin, about to be lured into the sleep of ages in a cave beneath the sea, frantically tries to recall if he had forgotten to tell the young Arthur anything. A vital bit of information could mean all the difference.

So it is that I think about Courtney's last phone call and wonder if I missed my one final shot at changing her fate.

Her favorite books were the *Chicken Soup for the Soul* series. She read them all and loved the warm stories with the happy endings.

I wish I could provide that for this book, too. But I can't change what happened, and healing, the end of the journey, comes only by weary increments.

Many mornings I still awaken and, as if for the first time, realize that Courtney is gone. It wasn't just a nightmare, or a dark thought that had flitted randomly across my mind. Her death was real, and the moment of comprehension cuts deep all over again like a chilling blade across my heart.

I don't often dream of her—at least, not that I recall. But one dream does remain clear in my mind.

On the last trip we all took together, Sherry, Jaime, and I stayed in a hotel in Manhattan, while Courtney visited a friend on Long Island. On the morning she joined us, she took a train to Grand Central Station and then cabbed it to the hotel.

She walked into the lobby, lugging a suitcase that was almost as big as she was, rolling it forward with all her might.

In my dream, she and I are walking together, but I am the one hauling that heavy suitcase, straining to keep it moving. Courtney turns to me and says, "Dad, you know you don't have to carry that bag anymore."

Even in the midst of the dream, I knew that she meant it was time to lay down my grief and live up to my pledge to seize the good times of life before they pass.

It isn't always easy.

But I'm working on it, Snort. God knows I'm working on it.